Beyond THE
RED CARPET

Beyond THE
RED CARPET

The World of Entertainment Journalists

FRANCINE BROKAW

Sourced Media Books, LLC
San Clemente, CA

Sourced Media Books, LLC
20 Via Cristobal
San Clemente, CA 92673
www.sourcedmediabooks.com

ISBN–13: 978-1-937458-22-5
LCCN: 2012910461

Printed in the United States of America.

This publication is designed to provide entertainment value and is sold with the understanding that the opinions expressed herein do not necessarily represent those of the publisher and that the publisher is not engaged in rendering legal, accounting, spiritual, political, or other professional advice of any kind. If legal advice or other expert assistance is required, the services of a competent professional person should be sought.

—From a Declaration of Principles jointly adopted by a Committee of the American Bar Association and a Committee of Publishers and Associations

This book is dedicated to my family—most importantly, to my husband, Roy, who schlepps me to and from screenings and interviews; to my mother, who gave me a love of reading; to my sister, who is always there; and to my dad, who was my biggest supporter.

Contents

Introduction

When people hear that I am an entertainment journalist, they usually imagine a life of glitz and glamour: they envision me going to cocktail parties, decked out in stunning jewelry and designer dresses, and hobnobbing with A-listers over drinks and *hors d'oeuvres*. While I do enjoy a good cocktail party from time to time, people usually have a different vision of what I *actually* do for a living. As Kevin Costner once told a group of us, our friends probably think we lead glamorous lives because we attend Hollywood functions and are always with celebrities. However, just as acting is just a job for him, entertainment journalism is just a job for us. And though we do have some interesting experiences, the job requires a lot of work.

This book is written for people who are interested in the entertainment business and would like to learn more about Hollywood from an insider's perspective. In the following chapters, many of my colleagues from around the country relate their experiences about working in entertainment media. Some write for newspapers, magazines, and websites; others work in television or radio. We all work in the same business, but we have a variety of perspectives about entertainment journalism, specifically, and Hollywood, in general.

While our perspectives differ, there is one thing on which we can basically agree: we love our jobs. So, for anyone interested in what it is like to be on the other side of the entertainment business, read on. We just might surprise you.

1

Beginnings

I never thought about being an entertainment journalist. I wanted to be a political speech writer, to make an impact on the world with words. I was astounded at the power that words had to revolutionize society throughout our history: "Give me liberty or give me death"; "Four-score and seven years ago"; "Ask not what your country can do for you. Ask what you can do for your country"; "I have a dream"; "Some people see things as they are and say, 'Why?' I dream things that never were and say, 'Why not?'" Phrases like these marshalled support, called people to action, and literally changed the world. I wanted to be part of it.

As we all know, things don't always go according to plan. For quite a while, I wrote technology articles for MSN. My job consisted of testing new hardware and software, then writing up reviews. Unfortunately, the products didn't always work the first time, and I had to reformat my computer—a lot. It was tedious, time consuming, and extremely frustrating. Simply put, it was a pain in the neck.

After one particularly long day dealing with technology woes, I started thinking about other possibilities. I decided that since I was living in Los Angeles, the entertainment capital of the world, I would take advantage of it.

I called a local television station and asked to speak with David Sheehan, the entertainment reporter. David was a leader in Los Angeles entertainment broadcasting. As a matter of fact, he was the first television and movie interviewer/reviewer to be a regular on a daily news broadcast. I explained my situation and asked for his guidance. He immediately had his assistant email me a list of studio contacts and gave me a few hints. I started making the calls, and the rest is history.

This job does not come with instructions. We pretty much have to figure it out on the fly. In the beginning, we hang on by the seat of our pants; but, as we become more and more entrenched in the business, we discover our own ways of doing our jobs. Many of my colleagues have backgrounds in film or journalism. Some studied film in school and, because of that, have different perspectives when viewing a movie. I have a background in English and have always enjoyed going to movies and watching TV. So I write from the perspective of a viewer. My reviews do not have descriptions of camera angles or specifics about the special effects; instead, I concentrate on the entertainment experience of the viewer at the movie. After all, don't most people go to movies to be entertained?

To be good at this job, you have to have realistic expectations of celebrities. The first rule of entertainment journalism is not to put actors on pedestals. They are just people doing their jobs, but the difference is that they work in front of an audience. Like everyone, they complain about the hard work their jobs entail. They spend a lot of time waiting for their scenes and reading their scripts. And they have to endure volatile swings of public opinion. But I wonder how many of them would change places with a roofer or a street paver in the middle of summer? To stay grounded, I remind myself that actors and filmmakers are regular people doing their jobs, and they are not more important than anyone else.

For the most part, entertainment journalism is "hurry-up-and-wait," combined with five minutes of usable information, added to hours of sitting in traffic, blended together with days of transcribing. When I first began the job, I accepted every—and I mean every—screening invitation. It was new, after all. My husband and I went to several movies a week. The first couple of awards seasons were brutal. We had to see several films in one day, and, of course, they were in different parts of the city, which meant we spent hours driving in traffic. Then, after seeing the movies, I took the notes that I had written during the films (writing in the dark is not the optimal way to jot down information, by the way), then spent additional hours writing cohesive articles, features, and reviews.

In addition to reviewing movies, books, and other media, entertainment journalists also interview celebrities. The celebrity interview is sometimes similar to the interview scene in *Notting Hill* (with Julia Roberts and Hugh Grant). Hugh Grant's character is mistaken as a journalist in a hotel suite waiting (with many journalists) to interview Julia Roberts. When it is his turn, he is ushered into another room for a face-to-face interview. Sometimes we get a face-to-face interview, but much of the time, we participate in roundtables and press conferences with a few phone calls scattered into the mix.

The journalists on the evening entertainment shows do things a little differently, but they are only a minute percentage of my colleagues. They still do their share of grunt work, but at the end of the day, they are coiffed and dressed—and look red-carpet ready. The majority of us are somewhat faceless. When we do our jobs, we are not made up by professional hairstylists and makeup artists. We simply go home, do our work, and that's that. So, when you see those beautiful entertainment journalists on television telling you about the latest movie or what happened to a specific actor that day, just remember they are a very small minority of entertainment journalists.

I should also clear up one thing before going on: the subject of freelance writing. Being a "freelancer" is not anything to look down upon. Actually, the majority of writers are freelancers. This simply means they are not full-time "staff." It doesn't mean that they don't work as hard as staff writers. On the contrary, oftentimes they must work even harder in order to lock down an outlet to publish their work. Many freelancers are connected to a specific outlet but are just not on staff. A lot of writers begin as freelancers and are later hired on as full-time staff writers. Many publications (both print and online) rely on freelance writers for their content. So during the course of this book, when you read about freelance writers, keep in mind that they are as valuable and respected in the world of entertainment journalism as those who are staff writers for specific publications.

I look back on my career in entertainment journalism with satisfaction. It's not exactly what I had envisioned doing with my life, but I have had some amazing experiences. And as you will read in the following pages, my colleagues agree. They have varied histories and stories about how they landed the jobs that they hold. Some have come from different departments at newspapers, others had never been in journalism before starting their jobs in this field, and still others have worked in other aspects of the entertainment business. For this chapter, I asked them to answer the question, "How did you get started in the business?" Though there are many paths to the world of entertainment journalism, we have one thing in common: we enjoy what we do. It's a difficult job, but there are some good payoffs. Plus, we have lots of great stories to tell at parties.

David Sheehan, Hollywood Close-Ups, Inc.

How I got started in the entertainment business is too long of a story to relate here. But the essence is that I had an early yearning to write about famous people and entertainment events as a boy in Columbus, Ohio, where I successfully talked my way onto the local paper's "stringer" staff covering sports. From there, I went to Notre Dame and got similar work in South Bend, followed by a transfer to UCLA and yet more newspaper and magazine jobs. That led to my fascination with theater and the establishing of my own rep company in L.A. and San Francisco doing the best of Jules Feiffer and Edward Albee and Harold Pinter, etc. The frustration of not being able to get any coverage on the various TV news programs (since they had no entertainment reporters in 1970) led me to propose the idea to all three network stations (cold and unsolicited in the mail, with my newspaper credentials, of course), and all three were interested. I chose CBS and began on KNXT (now KCBS) in 1971 as a movie reviewer and entertainment reporter—the first in TV history on a regular newscast.

George Pennacchio, KABC-TV

I blame it all on my mom and her never-ending supply of movie magazines. I knew far too much about movies and movie stars as a young child. Yeah, after I finished reading the back of the cereal box in first grade, I was thumbing through movie magazines. That, I'm sure, sparked an early interest in movies. I'd already fallen in love with a thing called television; and, since I had afternoon kindergarten, my bedtime when I was five was eleven o'clock, so I watched the networks' primetime line-ups every night—usually for all three hours.

Those are the memories, I believe, that set me on my way, although I didn't quite know it then. I would go on to be the editor of my high school and college newspapers. Then, after one day on the job at WMAQ-TV as an intern, I knew television news was my future. It took a while to get exactly where I wanted to be, but my years as a TV news producer ended up being great preparation for working fast and accurately in a business of constant deadlines.

In a nutshell, I was hired in Chicago after college and stayed there until I got a producing gig in Monterey. Once there, I suggested that I also do entertainment. The boss said, "Okay, but you're not getting any extra money." That didn't matter to me. I moved on to San Diego to produce the news again and, once again, convinced the boss I could do entertainment. He said, "Okay," too, and I did two jobs there for many years until I got a call from KABC-TV in Los Angeles. I've been the entertainment reporter here since 1996.

Howard Benjamin, Interview Factory Radio Networks

Right out of high school I went to work as a disc jockey for KHJ FM (now known as KRTH FM) radio in Los Angeles, California. It was the sister station to KHJ AM, a.k.a. "Boss Radio," the most listened-to station in the western half of the U.S. It was a case of being in the right place at the right time. At first, it was part time, but it soon grew into a full-time position. As an on-air personality, I started interviewing recording artists on my show. I did this while pursuing a college degree in design at Woodbury College. Before I knew what I was doing, it became clear that I was becoming an entertainment journalist.

Brian Sebastian, Movie Reviews & More

I never thought about being in the business. It's something that just happened. I used to run three video stores in Southern California, and a lot of celebrities used to come in. I would always give them my picks of movies that suited their tastes. They loved how I was able to pick movies that they liked. I never wasted their time.

Rick Bentley, *Fresno Bee*

I studied English and art in college but never had any interest in teaching. My jobs while in college were school photographer and editor of the yearbook. I also worked part time at a local print shop where I learned a lot about design.

When I heard the *Kentucky New Era* had an opening for a sports writer, I thought, "I can do that." Luckily, my skills with a camera and a willingness to work cheap kept me employed as I worked on my writing.

Sean Daly, *New York Post*

I kind of fell into the business in college. When I was a freshman at Syracuse University, I met a publicist for the biggest concert promoter in the Northeast. He offered to give me tickets to any show I wanted to see in exchange for writing some pre-show stories on the acts. This was in the mid-1980s. So I spent the next few years pitching my interviews with Duran Duran and Tina Turner to daily newspapers in cities like Albany, Syracuse, and Buffalo. I would write the same story for each and change just one or two sentences to make it local to each city. Then I would fax it to the editors. Before long I had about a dozen newspapers in my own little syndicate. Years later, after taking time off to get into a completely different line of work, I returned to journalism. By then I had moved to Los Angeles, where I actually was near some of the people I wanted to write about. (No more phoners or having to wait until their tour came to town.)

In 1999, I tried to get "hired" by a newspaper or magazine in L.A. but found the competition was fierce, and my clips were now ten years old. So I started my own publication: *Showtime Magazine*. I wrote most of the stories, laid it out on my Mac, and drove out to Ontario, CA to have it printed. My "other" job was in the restaurant business in Santa Monica, so I knew a lot of business owners who supported me with local ad dollars. I paid for the balance out of my own pocket. It was a good investment. Before long we were able to get into a few junkets and get access to real celebrity interviews, which I then repurposed and started selling back to many of the same newspapers I worked for so many years earlier.

Eventually I got an agent who hooked me up with a few bigger papers, and in 2001, I was hired as a freelancer at *Us Weekly*. I continued to work for the other newspapers but folded *Showtime Magazine*. (I no longer needed it.) I would interview an actor like Tom Cruise, write about him in six or seven local newspapers (as I had done years earlier), and then sell the transcript of my interview to *Us* or *People* or *In Touch* or whoever, for big bucks. They would cut it up and use quotes in stories or photo captions or find small news items in there. It was a win-win for everyone. Over the years, I bounced around (sometimes on staff and sometimes under contract) to *In Touch*, *Star* magazine, TMZ, *Toronto Star*, and most recently, *The New York Post*.

Rob Owen, *Pittsburgh Post-Gazette*

In the fall of 1989, I was attending college at Syracuse University, and I wrote up a preview of the new shows in the fall television season. I walked it up to *The Daily Orange*, which is a student-run campus paper. I figured they wouldn't want it but offered it to them anyway. I was a little naive and didn't realize at that point that campus newspapers are desperate for any copy of quality. They took the story and ran it. I ended up becoming the TV and movie critic for the next four years and eventually Features Editor at the paper.

Bonnie Siegler, Freelance

When I moved to Los Angeles from Upstate New York, I discovered my Bachelor of Science degree was not reciprocal for medical work in California and would require additional hours of schooling. Since I moved out West with just $500 in my pocket, enrolling in school again was not an option. I had minored in journalism in college and always liked the written word, so I parlayed that skill with my current job within an entertainment business management firm in order to make connections. My first big sale was to *Family Circle*.

Jacqueline Cutler, Tribune Media Services

I fell into entertainment writing when I did a freelance piece for a former editor. My first piece was a Q and A with Miss Piggy.

Before that I had done fifteen years in hard news. I love new, and had covered a variety of beats, including cops in NYC, the state capitol, education, and general assignment. When my first child was born, I wanted to raise her and stay in the business, foolishly thinking I could always return to newspapers because they would always be there. But I was incredibly lucky that a former metro editor was working at what was then TV Data and asked me to write a piece, which led to more and more pieces and a staff job twelve years ago.

Donna Plesh, Thecolumnists.com

When the paper I was working for as a copy editor was beefing up its entertainment coverage, I thought writing about television would be an easy and fun job, so I made a pitch to the editor and got the job. I soon discovered it was *not* an easy job!

Tim Riley, *Woodland Daily Democrat*

I started 30 years ago when living in Sonoma and discovered the local paper did not cover entertainment. I offered to write film reviews to get in the door.

Valerie Milano, *Hollywood Today*

Living in the entertainment capital makes the industry accessible and appealing. The glamour and celebrities have always intrigued me. Getting involved with the Television Critics Association (TCA) nineteen years ago was when I really began my best writing.

Mike Reynolds, Veteran Entertainment Journalist

At one month shy of my sixteenth birthday, I joined the Royal Air Force. In the living quarters, above an entrance door was a speaker with two knobs: one for volume, the other for changing stations. While the staid old BBC could be found on two of the three choices, the other choice was something none of us had ever heard—and no one ever managed to work out what station it was. After two days, we didn't have uniforms yet, and in the line for breakfast I stood behind someone in uniform. Guessing he knew everything (as he had been there long enough to get a uniform), I tapped him on the shoulder and asked if he knew what the non-BBC station was. He told me it was Forces Radio. I asked where they were located, thinking it would be London (we were a long way from London), but he pointed to an unmarked door across the corridor. "There," he said.

After the evening meal, I decided to go look, so I knocked on the door. I just wanted to see what a radio station was like. The door opened about three inches, and a voice asked, "What do you want?" From out of nowhere, I heard my reply, "I want to be on the radio." Where did that come from? I had never even thought of it, let alone had the nerve to ask, but somehow it came out.

A laugh came from behind the door, along with a "Well, you'd better come in." The door fully opened, and a man welcomed me to the station. For the next few minutes, he showed me every room of the station, explaining that it would take a very, very long time for anyone to get on the air because of all the preliminary training one would have to go through. The final room he took me to was the studio where a DJ was live on-air. What a rush! What a feeling, to be in an actual studio when someone was broadcasting to an audience! I was introduced once the DJ had announced the next record and was off-air. We had a brief chat, then he had to ready his next record. We shook hands, and I exited the studio.

"You can hang around if you want," the man told me.

I went to the record library and was just amazed at the number of records available in all their alphabetized boxes. I had entered the station just a few minutes after 6:00 P.M. It was now 7:27, and the man who had guided me around the station entered the library.

"Didn't you want to be on the radio?"

"Yes!"

"Well, you'd better grab some records. You're on at 7:30."

And so began my career—thanks to a man who turned out to be the station manager and who had given me his nightly show, though he never explained why he had had the courage to do so. To be honest, I never asked him. I was just too happy to be on-air each night.

Meg Mimura, *Lighthouse*

When I moved to L.A., I thought I wanted to be an entertainment publicist. My career counselor thought I'd be perfect because I am bilingual (English and Japanese) and bicultural. However, as suggested by her, I took the UCLA Extension class, Entertainment Public Relations, to see if I liked it. In the second class I realized that being a publicist is just like being a lawyer. I can't promote a show I don't believe in. I'm too honest to be a publicist, and it's not in my nature to pretend! So back to the drawing board.

That's when I examined all the Japanese magazines published here in L.A. The "Aha!" moment was that each magazine had a film critic of its own, but nobody was writing about TV shows. I used to recommend TV shows to my Japanese friends who lived in L.A., and they all loved them. They would come back for more because there were just too many shows to choose from. I think the sheer number of shows available on TV intimidates non-English speakers. It was an easy choice; I have always loved watching TV. You could say I've always been a TV addict. It was a great escape from harsh reality when I was growing up in Japan. I was bullied and didn't want to go to school. I tolerated those mean nuns and bullies during the day and then ran home to turn on TV and escape into a seemingly wonderful world of U.S. dramas and sitcoms! Yes, I did find out those worlds didn't exist at all, but still, I so enjoyed a brief relief from my miserable existence in Japan.

I quickly made a course correction, and the funny thing was that once I knew for sure I wanted to be a TV critic, everything just fell into place beautifully. Like Coach Taylor (played by Kyle Chandler) says in *Friday Night Lights,* "Clear eyes, full hearts, can't lose!"

My big break came when a Los Angeles-based Japanese magazine did a feature piece on me as a Japanese woman pursuing the American Dream. At that point, I was a member of the Academy of Television Arts & Sciences and worked on two movies while working my way into the TV arena. The editor who interviewed me was so impressed with my "They can only say no" attitude that she practically gave me a full page to play with. I managed to convince her that behind-the-scenes stories are more interesting than ordinary series reviews and started interviewing anybody who was willing to spend some time talking about their shows or roles.

Stephen Whitty, *Star-Ledger*

I was actually very interested in film criticism as a child. I was reading Pauline Kael in grade school, amassing my own little index cards of film reviews. I even wrote a history of horror films. I always thought I'd be writing for films, though, not about them.

Gerri Miller, Freelance

I got my first job as an assistant at *16 Magazine* in New York and spent almost four years there learning the biz. From there I went to Sterling-Macfadden as an editor, working on movie/TV and music titles. I've been freelance since 1998.

Candace Havens, FYI Television

It wasn't a job I ever thought would be possible when I was younger. When I was in journalism school, I always wanted to be a film or television critic, but my professors always said those jobs were few and far between.

I answered an ad in a newspaper about writing for a cable guide. I don't know why the editor hired me, but I'm really glad he did.

Scott Pierce, *Salt Lake Tribune*

I never thought about it much. I was a happy assistant sports editor at the *Deseret News* (in Salt Lake City), which already had a television critic, Joe Walker. He wasn't much older than I was, and I never imagined he'd be leaving.

I was friendly with my predecessor at the *Deseret News*. We used to talk TV quite a bit. (Naturally.) This was the late 1980s, when prime-time soaps were still hugely popular. I liked them and Joe didn't. So I used to write a few things about *Dallas, Dynasty, Knots Landing,* etc., for him.

When Joe left the paper and the job opened up, I jumped at the chance to be the TV critic. I was one of many applicants inside and outside the paper and somehow managed to land the job. That was March of 1990.

Todd Gilchrist, Freelance

I was writing reviews as far back as eighth grade, when I reviewed *The Abyss* for my junior high newspaper. I did a little bit of writing in high school, but it wasn't until college that I really started to find my niche, after I started at the school paper as a political cartoonist and ran out of ideas after about two days. After graduating, I did some professional writing for a number of weekly publications; but, when I ran into a buddy in Los Angeles about a month after I moved there, and he happened to be the editor of a local weekly, I really got what I'd call my official start doing entertainment reporting on a regular basis.

Michael Lee, RadioFree.com

I had been interested in writing since grade school after being introduced to *The Chronicles of Narnia* and *The Lord of the Rings*.

By junior high I had started to write short stories, even going so far as to submit content to publishers, but never considered a writing career in anything beyond fiction. It wasn't until I discovered the world of film junkets that I even looked into a life of reporting.

Technically, the first film junket I covered was in the year 2001 for *Session 9*. At the time, I thought it was merely a one-time promotional anomaly to publicize a film beyond the typical screening and movie review, and I never looked into the existence of similar events. It wasn't until 2004, when I randomly received an invite from The Angellotti Company (a PR firm), that I began to cover junkets regularly. That invite eventually led to covering Focus Features' *The Door in the Floor*, which I consider my first "official" junket. Shortly thereafter, I made blanket requests to publicists from a variety of studios and PR firms without really knowing the politics or hierarchy involved. As a result, I probably made far bolder requests than I would now. In retrospect, that fearlessness was probably a good thing that got me through a few doors—when you're blissfully ignorant, you have no fear of rejection.

Julio Martinez, *VIP Latino Magazine*, KPFK Radio

In 1972, I was touring as the accompanist/arranger for singer Al Jarreau. We were being booked all over the Midwest and Canada as the opening act for a number of big-name talents like Bill Cosby, Jefferson Airplane, Steppenwolf, etc. Al and I would split $500, and the name act would usually get around $10,000. A friend of mine who worked at *Rolling Stone* thought this was appalling and asked Al to write a story about it. Al didn't want to do it, but I did. It was published, and I thought this could be a fun gig. In 1982, years after I had stopped touring, I took my article to the editor of *Drama Logue*, and he hired me to write a weekly Cabaret column. That was my first job as an entertainment journalist.

Fred Topel, Crave Online

When I was in eighth grade, I started writing movie reviews for the middle school paper. I continued that through college but never really thought about it as a profession until 1999 when I moved to L.A. I just didn't know it was possible. When I saw that I could go to the red carpets and interview the stars, I thought that sounded like the perfect job for me.

I started writing for websites and then pitched myself to the studios so I could cover their premieres for those sites. I got some good interviews on the red carpet back in the day and was able to sell more and more stories—the more I went out and interviewed celebrities. Then I heard about the magical world of junkets, where you could actually spend 20 minutes interviewing someone, not just two minutes as they walk by!

Winnie Bonelli, North Jersey Media Group

Like most people, I was intrigued by show business celebrities, but never really thought about writing as a career.

I was a member of the Junior Woman's Club and volunteered to do the publicity by contacting local newspapers and writing press releases. A community newspaper approached me about doing a weekly column on local people, and my very first byline was a profile on Alan Alda, who resided in Leonia, NJ and was starring in *M*A*S*H*. I was totally smitten. Alda is articulate, funny, and intelligent. He also put me in touch with friends like the late author Robert Ludlum and television critic Marvin Kitman. Not long afterward, the locally published daily, *The Hudson Dispatch*, approached me about being a stringer. Along with features on prominent and not-so-prominent residents, there were borough council meetings, drownings, fires, and spot news. My kids were young, and I was able to juggle my work schedule with motherhood.

This eventually evolved into a full-time gig as "Action Reporter," settling consumer disputes, finding long-lost relatives, and retrieving money. Unfulfilled and bored, I started writing entertainment stories in addition to three weekly columns. *The Hudson Dispatch* had sister dailies in Trenton, NJ, Easton, PA, and Worchester, MA. My stories were running in four papers. Instead of prestigious, I used to joke that I was "free help." It did, however, provide the clout I needed to break into movie, television, and music fields.

Aaron Barnhart, *Kansas City Star*

In 1994, I began writing an Internet newsletter called *Late Show News* and giving it away on Usenet as well as through two online communities: *The WELL* and *ECHONYC*. People responded immediately to my first issue, which was a collection of items plus my commentary on the then-hot late-night talk show wars. Within three weeks the *Village Voice* was in touch about writing freelance for them.

Margie Barron, *Production Update*

I started thinking about being an entertainment journalist when I was in junior high in the '60s. The local paper had a very small staff, and when I would ask them to write about the shows at our school, they encouraged me to write the stories. Contributing stories to the paper continued in high school. I enjoyed entertainment stories the most.

In the early '70s, I got a big boost when I started to work in the marketing/PR department at the Playboy Club and Resort in Great Gorge, NJ, and I had to write our entertainment press releases for the New York/New Jersey area newspapers. Most would run the stories as I wrote them. Sometimes I would interview the entertainers that would be appearing in the showroom, and write the stories. Although I did take a journalism course in college, I learned more from actually doing the work than from listening to someone describe how the work should be done.

Alex Strachan, *Postmedia News*

I worked my way up at the local newspaper—the last of a dying breed—starting out as a copy boy and then eventually moving to sports, cityside, and finally entertainment. I came into the job as a fully rounded reporter, having covered everything from murder scenes, traffic accidents, and city council meetings to basketball games on deadline to general features. I applied for the entertainment beat when it came up in part because I was getting worn out from covering real-life tragedies.

Dave Walker, *New Orleans Times-Picayune*

I'd always had an interest in popular culture and was working as a feature writer when the opportunity came open to write about TV. It's the broadest possible specific newspaper beat, and the field of topics swings wide. Column subjects in a typical month range from serious to silly. Cable and broadcast TV, and now Internet-delivered programming, delivers every kind of subject.

Hanh Nguyen, TVGuide.com

Confession time. I never wanted to be a journalist. Okay, that's not quite true. I was on the staff of my middle school newspaper but instantly became disillusioned by the rather narrow scope and requirements of this job. My particular brand of curiosity did not lend itself to stories about school lunches, and my voice was obliterated with the excruciating minutiae of counting characters and hyphenating correctly. I took the school by drizzle, which quietly, anonymously, fizzled to the point I can't remember ending my tenure there.

That said, I always knew I was a writer. Words just plague me too much. With my handy creative writing degree in tow, I moved from Houston, Texas to Los Angeles with my then-roommate, who had just graduated with a communications degree. After working as a background extra (you may have seen me during the Halloween episode of *Felicity* or in *Saved by the Bell: The New Class*), I became a PR assistant at the Carsey-Werner Production company (home of such illustrious sitcoms as *The Cosby Show, Roseanne, 3rd Rock from the Sun,* and *That '70s Show*). There, I learned how to eat dessert (they provided chef-prepared lunches every day to employees) and that publicists have the most thankless job. When the company downsized, I was among the second wave of layoffs.

It was at that point I determined that the next job I took, no matter how small, had to get me closer to writing and language. I landed a part-time gig as a proofreader while I wrote for free on a website called *Sexy Monkey*, which I believed had a readership comprised of its staff of four. There, I waxed prophetic on who was the worst Olsen twin and how watching *The Red Balloon* as a child only reinforced my lifelong automaton phobia. These two gems were among the writing samples I sent in to an ad I found on Craigslist. Somehow, this company was unafraid of my obvious quirks and called me in. After performing an in-house writing test, I got hired in 2003.

In short, my path to entertainment journalism: bookworm childhood, procrastinating essayist, grammar tutor, bank patron No. 8 on *News Radio,* paid intern, unpaid writer, movies and TV journalist.

Rob Salem, *Toronto Star*

It was a total accident. I dropped out of high school to be an actor. I took Second City workshops with John Candy and Joe Flaherty and extra work on SCTV, hoping to get into the touring company.

I got sidetracked (Candy's idea) into stand-up comedy. I was working as a night-shift copyboy here at the *Star* to support my showbiz "career." Eventually I pestered the Entertainment editor into letting me freelance, starting with a story about . . . stand-up comedy.

It sucked. But I guess I got better. That's an old newspaper tradition—working your way up from copyboy. Now you need to be top of your class at journalism school and be sleeping with the Managing Editor, let alone be in possession of a valid high-school diploma. But hey, it was the '70s.

The paper's distinguished film critic saw *Animal House* and realized that was the immediate future of contemporary cinema. So I, being the only guy in the newsroom with an earring, got to be back-up film critic with absolutely no qualifications at all except my lack of age and any discerning taste in popular film.

About fifteen years ago, I was transferred (very much against my will) to the TV beat. It took me a while to realize that this was my first, best destiny, and that I had been preparing for it since toddler-hood.

This also happened to be the precise moment that television suddenly became the place to be, creatively, as *The Sopranos* and *Six Feet Under* and *Sex and the City* changed the entire medium.

2

Misconceptions

So, you think being a Hollywood critic, journalist, or writer is all fun and games? Think again. The vision most people have about entertainment journalists is that we wear beautiful clothes and spend all our time at Hollywood parties schmoozing with actors and filmmakers. Wouldn't that be the life? If that were actually the case, my job would be even more difficult, because everyone and their cousin would want to be doing what I do. This job entails a lot more than schmoozing with George Clooney and Angelina Jolie. It requires intelligence, wit, tenacity, time, a way with people, a way with words, and a lot of hard work. Yes, you read correctly. It is *work*, plain and simple! Well . . . there is a *little* play, there *are* some fun times, and we *do* get to go to special events. But work is at the core of this job. This is probably the largest misconception people have about entertainment journalism.

I was reminded of this misconception when my niece visited me one weekend. I had a junket for a film starring Dermot Mulroney and decided to take my niece along with me. I had planned on having her spend time in the press room, where publicists congregate, often with the actors. I thought this would be a fun experience for her. The studio publicist (a very nice man who always goes above and beyond his duty) offered my niece a place in my roundtable, which meant she would be able to watch the interview.

The interview went well, and my niece was excited to have been there. On the way home, she called her friends and told them that she spent the morning with Dermot Mulroney. We got home, and she went to take a nap. I, on the other hand, spent the entire afternoon transcribing the interviews. (Transcribing the taped conversation takes more time than the actual interview. I listen to a sentence over and over again, making sure I have not left out a word or substituted a word for what was said. It's really a daunting task.) The next day, I wrote up my articles. So what was simply a fun morning for my niece was two days of work for me.

A second misconception is that celebrities always like publicity. Not true. If they don't have a product to promote (i.e., movie, TV show, perfume line, etc.), they simply want to be left alone. One time, I had a magazine cover story ready to go. It had already been submitted, along with photos of the actress I was interviewing. The cover and inside photos were provided by the studio publicity department, because the actress was co-starring in a new film. I had interviewed her the previous week and had written a flattering and informative article about this actress's life, career, and family.

At about six o'clock in the evening, I received a phone call from the actress's personal publicist informing me that I was to pull the cover photo and story. *What?* It didn't make any sense. She insisted I call the magazine and pull the story, because she hadn't been the one to supply the photo for the cover. I explained that the photo was very nice and was supplied by the studio. The article was complimentary and included nothing harmful about the actress or the movie. Again, she insisted I pull the story.

I was angry. I had not done anything wrong, yet this publicist was rude and condescending. I couldn't have pulled the story even if I wanted to—the magazine was already at the printer. Needless to say, I didn't write up any more stories about her clients. If she wanted publicity for them, she would have to approach me again. She never has.

A third misconception is that celebrities are always classy. The thing that first struck me when I began interviewing celebrities was how they presented themselves. Many of them would show up for interviews in T-shirts and ratty jeans. Sometimes they would bring in a can of beer. Years ago, studio bosses like Jack Warner would not have let their celebrities go to interviews dressed like slobs. But today is the time of ratty jeans and unkempt hair. Veteran actors always look and act professional, but some of the young actors feel they do not need to take any extra care in their presentation.

Sometimes celebrities act unprofessionally as well. I often get the feeling that they would rather be getting a root canal than be at a press event (sorry if I offend any dentists). I have seen several actors walk in one door of a cocktail party, through the room, then out the back door. They apparently feel that by making an appearance they have done their duty. We journalists feel otherwise.

A fourth misconception is that we are friends with the celebrities we interview. Not true. I have interviewed hundreds of celebrities and have yet to be invited over to their house for dinner! This is a concept many outside of the business miss. The day after interviewing Johnny Depp for *Pirates of the Caribbean*, I was at a party. The word got out that I had recently interviewed Johnny Depp. Soon, people were coming over to ask me about the actor. Before I knew it, people were saying that I was personal friends with Johnny Depp. The lesson here is that those celebrities we interview are not our friends, although once in a while some of us actually do know these people on a "friendlier" basis.

Okay, I admit that there are some wonderful things I get to do for my job. It's not all work. But it definitely involves more than partying, attending events, going to free movies, talking with celebrities, and collecting fun stories to tell my friends. This misconception and others are evident in the interviews I conducted with my colleagues. For this chapter, they were asked the question, "What are the biggest misconceptions people have about your job?" We all agree that life inside Hollywood is not all glitz and glamour, but it does have its moments!

Mike Reynolds, Veteran Entertainment Journalist

That I am "lucky enough" to get to see every movie and review every TV show and album I want for free. That I have hundred of celebrity friends to have fun with. Oh, and that I hardly really "work." Well, I do see thousands of movies and TV shows and hear albums for free. But to get to the really good—the excellent—ones, I have to sit through so many bad ones, and the number of "lost hours" in life witnessing garbage is not fun at all.

Yes, I do get to travel to wonderful places, but I never really "see" them as I am there to work. So I often go from airport to hotel or location and then back to the airport.

No, I am not "best friends" with celebrities. I don't go to their homes all the time for social events, etc.

There is so much research going into every story and interview. No one understands that at all. The other thing, not a misconception but an unknown to the general public, is that this is a 24/7 profession. News does not happen between 9 A.M. and 5 P.M. Monday through Friday, so one is on call every single day of the year, every year!

George Pennacchio, KABC-TV

The biggest misconceptions? People think I pop into the TV station and read material that's been prepared for me before I go off on a four-hour dinner break, returning to read another segment for the eleven o'clock news. Really? I'm in by 1:30 P.M. every day (sometimes seeing movies or doing interviews at 11 A.M. first), writing with my producer for the four o'clock news, and then I'm generally off to shoot, write, and turn in a new story for the eleven o'clock news. I produce my own segment for the late news (all that news producing has done me well over the years). Bottom line: I work *a lot,* and it's definitely not a 9–5 Monday through Friday life. That doesn't exist in my world.

David Sheehan, Hollywood Close-Ups, Inc.

They have no way of knowing about the long hours of toil and torment in the editing room and at the word processor to make what you're doing as good as possible.

Hanh Nguyen, TVGuide.com

Oy. Where do I start? Entertainment is the product, but the job itself is not necessarily entertaining. The amount of hours it takes to write one piece—from viewing a screener/screening, researching questions of the talent, transcribing, constructing the feature, arguing with the editor over phrases and placement—overshadows the miniscule amount of time it takes to do the "entertaining" part, which is the all-too-brief interview.

For fun, a friend of mine who is not a writer volunteered to freelance as a recapper for my website. I actually told him upfront that he didn't have to volunteer, that I was just letting him know about the gig because it was one of his favorite shows. After one season of recapping, he reported back to me that he didn't want to do it anymore because, well, it was work. Yes, what did you think I was doing all these years?

Also, I really don't care about celebrities. I have never been starstruck, not even as a child. I did not have *Tiger Beat* posters (I was more into cute animals and superheroes) on my wall. When I am not working, I don't want to discuss Charlie Sheen. Even when I am working I don't want to discuss Charlie Sheen. Why, oh why, am I discussing Charlie Sheen now? Hmm . . .

It's hard to turn it off. Entertainment takes over your world, like some epinephrine-mainlining Stay Puft Marshmallow Man. Insomnia, one of my companions since childhood, has latched on and become codependent. Is it any wonder that my downtime is spent outdoors or with a nice, quiet book?

Margie Barron, *Production Update*

The biggest misconception about interviewing celebrities is that people will always ask, "What are the stars really like?" Well, just because you sit down with stars for about 30 minutes, and you ask them questions, and they are on their best behavior (usually), it doesn't mean you've really gotten to know them. But it does mean that you've gotten to know only what they want you to know.

Sometimes you can make a connection. And sometimes you can tell if they are being open and sincere. But that is rare. The truly great people in show business are those who see you over the years, and they remember you, and your interviews turn into conversations rather than questions and answers. Bryan Cranston is a truly great person, who remembers you, and cares about you, and sometimes he winds up asking more questions about you than you ask about him. What a guy.

Todd Gilchrist, Freelance

The biggest misconception is that it's possible to be "objective." I don't believe that objectivity exists, even in news reporting, so I admit I bristle when someone critiques me for being biased—especially when I write reviews. Everything comes from our point of view, and no matter how comprehensively we attempt to cover something, any act of narrowing our focus qualifies as subjectivity.

In a larger sense, I also think that the way in which entertainment reporting literally exists, it's nearly impossible to have an ongoing job as a reporter or journalist without engaging in some relationship at some level with the studios, publicists, and filmmakers who make the entertainment that we report on. That doesn't mean that people are inherently biased one way or another, but it requires reporters to create their own value system and their own ethics or the way they feel is appropriate to do their job. And ultimately, they have to find outlets and colleagues who share those values—and then they shouldn't worry about it, anymore.

Sometimes it's good to be reminded there are certain ways of doing things that either are or seem unethical, just to reinforce that what you're doing is right; but, as a rule, what I do as a journalist only reflects upon me, just as what my colleagues do reflects upon them. As a result, I can't worry about the larger ramifications of a person who's in my community who's doing something I don't like. It's a waste of effort and energy that could be applied to doing something for yourself.

Rick Bentley, *Fresno Bee*

The biggest misconception is shared by the public and many journalists. They think that just because I've done an interview, I have become close friends with the talent.

This is a business. I am there to get information for a story. The talent is there to promote their latest work. Nothing more.

I never assume that when I interview someone for a second time that they are even going to remember me. That's not important. All I want are the answers to use to do my job.

Tim Riley, *Woodland Daily Democrat*

People think that I hang out with celebrities and get invited to expensive parties. That seems to be only partially true during the TCA (Television Critics Association) TV Press Tour.

Jacqueline Cutler, Tribune Media Services

I am not sure what misconceptions people have. What people don't realize, I think, is how incredibly time-consuming it is to set up an interview. I am about to conduct a phoner with Simon Cowell, who should be calling any moment now. I have been working with publicists to set this up for ages, countless emails and calls—and he wants to do it! There is an awful lot of back and forth. I am not, so decidedly not, sitting in the back of a limo drinking champagne.

Brian Sebastian, Movie Reviews & More

People have no idea how much time we invest in our craft. I watched 1123 movies last year—1078 on home video alone. I still travel to film festivals and run around getting interviews instead of waiting for them to call me. It's nonstop. Movies open every Friday, and there is no down time like in the past.

Donna Plesh, Thecolumnists.com

Everyone (family members included) think I have a very "easy" job. Family and friends also think you get to hang out with celebs. They forget it is just a job, albeit different from, say, being an accountant and working 9 to 5. Again a misconception. It's not 9 to 5; it's when the talent is available for an interview, be it 5 A.M. to 10 P.M. And I also think accountants get paid a lot more!

Valerie Milano, *Hollywood Today*

Well, there definitely is a lot of glitz and glamour, but there really is quite a bit of pre-work before the legwork begins—setting up interviews and securing credentials to anything and everything going on locally and out of town. Research, note-taking, and keeping all of my things charged is always fun (camera, laptop, cell phone, Palm, Flip, recorder) and requires lots of batteries and technology to keep track of!

Sean Daly, *New York Post*

Most people do not understand the behind-the-scenes politics that are a daily part of our business—dealing with publicists who you know are lying to you, negotiating "exclusive" scoops, etc. Most people would probably be surprised how completely boring most celebrities are. The press (not counting paparazzi) are there to help these people sell their movies and TV shows and CDs to the public, but oftentimes they (celebrities) simply do not understand how to give a good quote or make themselves seem remotely interesting.

Stephen Whitty, *Star-Ledger*

People think I vote on the Oscars. I don't—it's for Academy members only. And that I go to all the premieres. I go to some when I have to but hate them as they always run at least an hour late. They also often think I'm friends with the people I write about; not true (and I'd be leery of any journalist who said it was true, or wanted it to be). And, far from being glamorous, covering a festival (Toronto, Sundance, etc.) is a lot of sixteen- to eighteen-hour days. I almost always end up coming home with the flu.

Rob Owen, *Pittsburgh Post-Gazette*

I think the biggest misconception is that it's all fun. I'm not going to deny that there are fun aspects of it. It's great to go on the set of a TV show. It's great to attend premieres or parties or whatever. There is a lot of fun to be had there. But there's a lot of work, too. Any time you do an interview with a tape recorder, you have to transcribe it. That takes forever. It's monotonous and not fun. And for myself, because I have also covered local television in the different markets I've been in and covered it critically, that means writing reviews of newscasts and anchors and reporters and that sort of thing. You know, when you write about folks on the national level they may not call and yell at you, but when you write about folks on the local level, they will call and yell at you. It's not just all fun and set visits and premieres.

Howard Benjamin, Interview Factory Radio Networks

People think it's just a conversation and you can use your own curiosity to get you through. I found out very early in my career that preparation was the key to a great interview. So if I know I have been given an hour with a performer, I will spend, on average, eight to ten hours doing research. The old adage of "garbage in garbage out" is not only true, it's an interviewer's worst nightmare. If you don't know what to leave out of an interview, how will you know what to include?

Bonnie Siegler, Freelance

People think it's got to be so much fun interviewing famous people, and usually it is. What most don't realize is that a lot involves hurry up and wait: waiting for the celeb on a set or waiting around for a phone interview that doesn't happen or is ultimately postponed.

Gerri Miller, Freelance

That it's all glamorous hobnobbing with the famous. There's a lot of work that people don't see—arranging, planning, setting up interviews, then transcribing and writing the stories.

Scott Pierce, *Salt Lake Tribune*

That I get paid to watch TV. I actually get paid to write about TV, which requires watching it first. Although I do know of some critics who somehow skip that step.

I would say the other misconception is that we're somehow friends with the people we cover. Frankly, that's either just plain wrong—we both have jobs to do—or it is, in my opinion, unprofessional.

Candace Havens, FYI Television

I work all the time. Actors work many hours, too, so you have to be flexible if you want to talk to them. I do more phone interviews than I think most people realize.

Julio Martinez, *VIP Latino Magazine,* KPFK Radio

Most people think I get paid well for what I do, because I get to interview superstars like Tom Hanks, Steven Spielberg, and Salma Hayek. There is also a misconception that if a person is a star, he or she is always interesting and highly intelligent.

Michael Lee, RadioFree.com

I think the biggest misconception is one with which a lot of entertainment reporters would probably agree: the idea that it's not work, it's not difficult, and it's nothing but fun and games. Granted, it's a far easier job than many other lines of work. It's not the grueling physical labor of construction, nor is it the more inflexible world of numbers or science. But that's not to say it is completely without downside. There are constant deadlines, and very often reporters find themselves spending ever-increasing hours at their jobs at the expense of their personal lives. It's a perpetual 24-hour-a-day cycle, especially given the emergence of an insomnia-fueled world of never-ending news. It also takes an underappreciated experience and skill set to become a good interviewer, and it's not always a simple matter of having a conversation with someone, as many people might assume.

The best interviewers come up with an interesting angle and set up the talent to shine. In an ideal situation, the interviewer should be transparent enough to allow their subject to show a—hopefully—intriguing side of themselves to the fans, readers, and viewers. Unfortunately, there are too many monstrous egos in Hollywood, which speaks to another downside of the job: As with any group of co-workers, reporters come with the good and the bad. The bad in Hollywood are perhaps a particularly grotesque sample of humanity ranging from the attention whores to the unethical and duplicitous. Another misconception of the job is that it's a breeze to see so many free movies in a given year. I would argue that even the most fervent film fan occasionally likes the opportunity to step away from a screen and live in the real world. Is there anyone who enjoys sitting through a streak of ten bad movies?

Fred Topel, Crave Online

People think I do nothing but watch movies all day. I do watch a lot of movies, but most of my time is spent gathering interviews, preparing, or writing. I think people hear "entertainment journalist" and immediately think "movie critic"—and then only think about the watching part. I think it's a shame because there are even better aspects to my job than just watching movies. Watching movies is awesome, but meeting the people who make them is even better. Getting to ask them questions is even better, and getting to tell their story is the best part.

Winnie Bonelli, North Jersey Media Group

When all the planets line up, it's sheer fun, but there are plenty of inconveniences—like waiting for a Manhattan-bound bus when it's 10 degrees and snowing or arriving for an interview and being told there's an hour-and-a-half delay or the subject bailed at the last minute. Like most journalists, it's the passion for the job that helps us deal with the setbacks. It is much easier when you're on staff, whether it's a newspaper, magazine, online, or the radio, since you often call your own shots. But as a freelancer, you have to run everything past the editor, who may or may not agree with running a particular story.

Aaron Barnhart, *Kansas City Star*

That publicists cultivate us and lobby us. Outside of a handful of influential trade magazines and the *New York Times* and a couple other papers, they wait for us to get in touch with them— and then they often make it hard for us to get access, or the people they work with play hard to get.

Dave Walker, *New Orleans Times-Picayune*

I'm surprised and disappointed by how little time I can spend actually watching TV. Thanks to preview screeners and multiple DVRs, commercials aren't an issue. That would be hours in every week, lost. But I always tell people who ask that I actually watch less TV than the Nielsen average. . . . I don't keep up on every episode of every show, which people somehow think might be possible anyway. It's not.

Rob Salem, *Toronto Star*

That I spend all day flat on my back on the couch, shoveling Cheesies, with an orange-stained remote control inextricably clasped in my pudgy hand. Oh, wait, I do.

That, and that all the famous people I interview are close personal friends. I do nothing to dissuade that notion.

Alex Strachan, *Postmedia News*

The biggest misconception, ironically enough, is similar to the one facing sports reporters—everyone thinks it's about watching the game for free. No one realizes that once the game ends and they're going home, that's when your job begins. In entertainment that translates to, "You get to see movies for free," and they don't realize the actual work involved in forming a judgment, putting it into words, making it so those words make sense, and then trying to entertain the reader at the same time.

3

Competition

This is a highly competitive business, no doubt about it. It is competitive in several ways: there is competition between professionals, competition between types of media outlets, and competition between journalists and other online writers.

Many journalists are highly competitive. Some would not even think of helping out a colleague unless they got a byline credit or payment for it. However, many of my colleagues would do anything they could to help out another journalist. If I can help someone by asking an actor a special question (if my colleague cannot get an interview and I can), I am more than happy to do so.

Regardless of how helpful journalists are, the fact remains that there are countless websites filled with people who want to be "published" and a limited number of journalistic outlets. In order to make any headway as an entertainment journalist, you have to create relationships with network and studio publicists, as well as the publicists who work for all the publicity and PR groups. This requires making phone calls, writing emails, hustling, and schmoozing. Believe me, there are a lot of publicists out there—and if they know your name and the quality of your work, then you'll have a much easier time getting that elusive interview.

Finding a legitimate job as an entertainment journalist (not a "blogger") is very difficult, especially because there are fewer print outlets and the economy is in a recession. If you do manage to land a job in this field, you have to start at the bottom. You have to hustle, hustle, hustle. You cannot simply send out an article and hope someone sees how great it is. On the contrary, you have to continually be in contact with different publicists and make sure they know your name, so you will get that interview or inside information on a production. And you have to be good at what you do. Face it, if you can't write worth a damn, forget about it!

In addition to competition between professionals, there is much competition between media outlets. When I first began writing as an entertainment journalist, print, radio, and television outlets had priority. Now, online outlets often get the top recognition with studios. In the "old days," getting a "scoop" was great. That meant you got some information well before anyone else, and (in the era of print) once that information was printed, it was hours before another outlet would be able to print a similar article. These days, there really isn't anything to compare to that, unless you call "going viral" on the Internet a scoop.

Finally, there is a lot of competition between journalists and other online writers. There are a lot of people who write only for a byline, or to see free movies, or for the swag. They don't really care about the payment or their reputations and work for very little or no money. This hurts those of us who have made careers out of it.

Entertainment journalism isn't a business for the meek. It is a competitive business between professionals, between media outlets, and between journalists and other (especially online) writers. You have to work at this job. It isn't easy, but it is fun—most of the time.

Some people think of competition in this business as easier these days, because of the countless websites that need to be filled with content. But when you realize that there are countless websites that need to be filled with content—and a lot of writers flooding the business—then you see the competition for what it really is.

For this chapter, journalists were asked, "How competitive is this business?" As you will see, most of my friends in the business think of it as extremely competitive.

Donna Plesh, Thecolumnists.com

Very. There are many, many talented writers out of work in these tough economic times who have turned to freelance to make a living. Plus, there just is not a lot of freelance work out there these days.

Howard Benjamin, Interview Factory Radio Networks

In a word: Very! The longer I do this for a living, the more I'm struck by the fact that there isn't a living soul on the planet that wouldn't trade places with me in a second. That having been said, the other reality is that no matter how good you are at something, someone will come along and do it for less. It's not that we are talking Pulitzer prize-winning journalism, it's pure economics! Just when you think you're one of the chosen few, some upstart comes along and makes you look like a novice. The key is to never take what you do for granted and never be complacent.

Mike Reynolds, Veteran Entertainment Journalist

It never used to be competitive, in the "kill or be killed" sense; journalists would often share things with one another—as long as an exclusive had been put to bed and it was too late for the others to beat them. Often information would be shared, because one journalist needed more information on something. In those early days it was quietly competitive.

Today, however, it is far more cutthroat, and there are so many "journalists" who are not true journalists. Traditional journalism is a dying profession, and those traditional outlets are getting fewer and fewer. Adapting to the Web is fine, but the desire to be ahead of the game every second and doing so without the required fact-checking is causing so many problems and giving journalism a bad name—whether it's entertainment or hard-news journalism.

George Pennacchio, KABC-TV

The business is competitive in the sense that everyone wants to claim some "exclusive." At an awards show, one program may be the only one "in the hallway" after a star receives a trophy. Another one may be "the only camera backstage when the winner walks off stage." Someone else may have the only camera there "right before the stars meet the press." It just gets silly. I once did one of two interviews with a TV legend guest-starring on a hit show. A day or two later, a syndicated show was advertising that it was the only one on the set for the interview. Was I invisible that day?

Rick Bentley, *Fresno Bee*

That's something I try not to worry about. I have no control over whether a celebrity is going to say "yes" or "no" to me doing an interview. The only competition I have is with myself. I believe an entertainment reporter should be the chief source for readers when it comes to entertainment news. That means working hard to do everything I can.

Rob Owen, *Pittsburgh Post-Gazette*

I guess it depends on what it is you're going for. I certainly think it has changed with the advent of the Internet. I think it was probably much less competitive before the Internet, but now everyone wants their exclusive because exclusive means hits and getting picked up at aggregator sites and that sort of thing. I think competition has become fiercer than it once was. I think some people don't care about being the first with a story. I think they want to build a following and have people follow them because of the content of what they write and the thoughts that they have to express as opposed to being the first with the news.

Meg Mimura, *Lighthouse*

Very. I have to compete with not only Japanese film critics who live in L.A., but also all the bloggers who know nothing about TV but fake their way in. Since Japan is not buying as many films as they used to, local film critics started moving into my territory several years back. They can get away with glaringly incorrect information because studio publicists can't read Japanese. These people already have established relationships with publishers or networks, so it's really hard for a newcomer like me to replace them even with expertise in and passion for TV. It's a shame.

Bloggers tend to be outsiders who manage to get information from somewhere. The only selling point is the "speed." I can't compete with that, because I don't just gossip or whip up rough-and-ready articles.

I don't know how many print publications have gone out of business since I started, and like everywhere else in the world the publishing business looks bleak.

I guess the entertainment journalists' pie itself is getting smaller and smaller every year while more journalists, film critics, and bloggers are fighting over this ever-shrinking business. I don't know what the solution is.

Fred Topel, Crave Online

Extremely competitive. It's something everyone would love to do and many would do for free, so you've got to be really good to prove your work is worth paying for. Many of the people who do it may not realize how much competition there actually is, and they take it for granted. I make sure never to take work away from someone else. That's bad business. But you have to generate work for yourself.

Michael Lee, RadioFree.com

This may be a product of my fevered imagination, but I would say this business has gotten considerably more competitive since the time I started, if only because there are more outlets scrambling for the same story. I feel like it was easier to get exclusive content only three, four, or five years ago. It's also more competitive in terms of speed. With the advent of Twitter, Facebook, videos, and blogs, news is constant and instant. Curiously, this competitiveness has just about killed the quality of written news pieces. Rather than original editorials or stories, Internet outlets are obsessed with recycling and cannibalizing headlines amongst each other. "So and so broke this news, here's a link" has become a story in and of itself. There is also an increasing number of reporters who seem to be writing at a high-school level. I know this makes me sound like a dinosaur, but it's disheartening to see paid professionals crank out words that are indistinguishable from a cloud of tweets from kids.

Candace Havens, FYI Television

There are few jobs and many entertainment journalists/critics. It's extremely competitive.

Scott Pierce, *Salt Lake Tribune*

Because I'm not based in New York or L.A., I think my answer is probably different. In Salt Lake City, I was pretty much the only one chasing after this kind of stuff. And since I left the *Deseret News* (the minute they laid me off) for *The Salt Lake Tribune*, I genuinely don't have any competition. I've found that there's actually a lot of camaraderie among TV critics—at least with my friends. Everything from alerting each other about local angles to holding each other's tape recorders in scrums (the gathering of reporters around a celebrity) . . . and so on.

Gerri Miller, Freelance

Pretty competitive. Only the strong survive.

David Sheehan, Hollywood Close-Ups, Inc.

Well, the competitive edge is something that no doubt improves the quality of the work. But a lot of the competition is just minor paranoia about which reporter is in good favor with which member of management. This is with respect to TV news reporting, especially entertainment reporting. Of course, all aspects of show business are intensely competitive because nearly everyone would love to be a part of it.

Julio Martinez, *VIP Latino Magazine*, KPFK Radio

I only feel the competition at the TCA when I have to decide whether it is worth it or not to push through thirty or more TV critics to get a quote from J.J. Abrams!

Valerie Milano, *Hollywood Today*

This business is very competitive. There are print magazines, papers, blogs, reviews, and websites. Everyone has a question and an opinion; and in this town, any moment may offer an opportunity. So you must have a great question in your pocket.

Hanh Nguyen, TVGuide.com

In one sense, it is incredibly competitive, because I'm in the online world where information is instantaneous. Anyone can be a "reporter" these days without actually being a good writer or understanding actual journalism. The market is glutted. That being said, I try not to think too hard about what the other person is doing, but what I feel I should be doing for my company and career. Being competitive with myself is what's most important to me.

Sean Daly, *New York Post*

The business is extremely competitive—but at the same time not competitive at all if you know what you are doing and know who to talk to. People who send a resume and cover letter to *People* magazine will never in a million years get hired. Someone who calls up the bureau chief, introduces himself and says, "I can help you and here's how" can get hired on the spot. There is a huge misconception (at the top of the journalism food chain) that you are going to be able to interview a celebrity and write a story, and it will get published. That is almost never true. Newspaper, magazine, and TV editors/producers are looking for reporters, not writers. They need information, story leads, and pitches. You may get to do the big interview, but then someone else will write the story.

Margie Barron, *Production Update*

It can be terrible. I'm a very open person, and one time I was sitting next to a woman at a TCA Press Tour who was asking me questions about my main publication, and if I did any freelance work, and what outlets were freelance? I've always been proud of my outlets and told her. A few months later, I found out that she had contacted at least one of my magazines and underhandedly tried to take over the celebrity page I was doing.

Winnie Bonelli, *North Jersey Media Group*

It's extremely competitive, especially since so many of the outlets have dried up because of the economy. A lot of college-age kids are willing to work for free, so it's increasingly hard to make a decent salary. It's an occupation that you pursue because you love it, not to make money.

Tim Riley, *Woodland Daily Democrat*

I know it is competitive, but I have been writing for several smaller papers for so long that I don't feel tremendous pressure from competitors. It would be different if I were trying to tap into a new market.

Brian Sebastian, Movie Reviews & More

It's competitive if you're a writer or photographer, but I've never looked at it that way. I run around getting my interviews like a squirrel gathering nuts.

Alex Strachan, *Postmedia News*

Both more and less competitive than it used to be. Blogging, online, and Internet "journalism" has really crowded the field. But it's quantitative, not qualitative. The standard is so incredibly low for online journalism—shockingly, unforgivably low—that a decent writer can beat online bloggers just by stringing two or three coherent words together. The field is more crowded, but I wouldn't say it's more competitive. In my immediate area—western Canada and the Pacific Northwest—it was much more competitive when the *Seattle Post-Intelligencer*, *Seattle Times*, *Oregonian*, *Vancouver Sun,* and *Vancouver Province* all had their own TV critics. Now there's just one proper writer for the whole region, and a multitude of ignorant, uneducated, ill-informed, borderline illiterate writers who can barely think, let alone string together a proper sentence.

Todd Gilchrist, Freelance

This business is very competitive, as competitive as almost any other, because there are tons of people who would love to do what we are lucky enough to do—meet and interview celebrities and entertainers whose work we've enjoyed, sometimes for decades. Part of the reason it's so competitive, however, is because of the transition from print media to online, where few companies have created successful business models for payment of content. That's exacerbated by the willingness of new people to do the job for free (and companies to pay nothing) just for the opportunity to meet celebrities and entertainers, under the guise of "getting experience." The result of these two trends is the increased number of freelance writers trying to get the same work, as well as a decreased number of full-time staff positions doing this sort of writing.

Stephen Whitty, *Star-Ledger*

The competition for a longish, sit-down, one-on-one interview has gotten worse and worse, as press tours are shortened and studios try to do (and completely control) their own publicity more and more through Facebook, corporate blogs, etc. The competition to get into roundtable interviews and press conferences, though, has gotten easier and easier, which is bad in a different way, as more time is taken up by semi-amateurs lobbing softball questions, gushing fan-boy praise, or asking for snapshots and autographs.

Aaron Barnhart, *Kansas City Star*

It's not competitive—there are plenty of story ideas out there. What is lacking is access, and I believe among the so-called elite publications, there is a great deal of competition. However, since journalists like me have no chance of being invited to that card game, no worries.

Rob Salem, *Toronto Star*

Now? Are you kidding? With anyone with any kind of tenure getting sacked, and kids coming up willing to do four times as much work for a quarter of the money, and papers folding, and the Internet being perceived as actual journalism?

Dave Walker, *New Orleans Times-Picayune*

I suppose it's more competitive all the time, thanks to all the typing about TV that's happening out there on the Internet. The daily newspaper, a few magazines, and *Entertainment Tonight* were the only TV-covering entities when I started this. Mostly, I think I compete with everything everywhere for a reader's time. The audience for everything I write now is much larger than it's ever been thanks to my paper's affiliated website and the readers' ability to find what I've written via search. I spend a lot of time preparing blog posts to mine that curiosity, which is mechanical and not at all fulfilling, but essential. I started in this business as a copy boy, and one of my jobs was inputting late-night race results from the Phoenix dog track. Preparing blog posts requires the same level of creative energy, which is very little.

Strange Interviews

When preparing for an interview, we often have expectations about how the meeting will proceed. Sometimes the interviews live up to our expectations, sometimes they exceed them, and sometimes they fall flat.

Press day for the 2004 film *Ocean's Twelve* comes to mind. Because of the large cast and the popularity of each member of the cast, Warner Bros. did not offer roundtables or one-on-one interviews. Instead, they held press conferences at the Bighorn Country Club, an upscale resort in Palm Desert near Palm Springs. The producer, Jerry Weintraub, had a home there. The journalists were scheduled to meet at a hotel in the area, then we were bussed to the exclusive country club.

We had been to a screening of the film the night before on the Warner Bros. lot. Most of us had high expectations about the press day. After all, there were some pretty big names in the film—George Clooney, Brad Pitt, Matt Damon, Catherine Zeta-Jones, Julia Roberts, Andy Garcia, Don Cheadle, and others—although not all of them were scheduled to attend the press day. I was expecting to be able to get at least six good feature articles from the press junket.

The large cast was divided into two groups, so we had two press conferences. Six or seven actors attended each press conference, which made it difficult to get much information from any one person. To make things even more difficult, the actors did not take the press conference seriously and continually joked among themselves, leaving the journalists with very little to write. The actors were entertaining (think of the Rat Pack in Las Vegas); but they didn't give us much information for our articles. In the end, I was hard-pressed to get even one interesting and cohesive article from the couple of hours I spent at the press conference. Except for the entertainment value of listening to the actors banter back and forth, the morning was a bust.

As we left the resort, many of us complained to each other, and when we arrived back at the hotel where we began the day, our frustration was clear to those who were waiting for us. My husband, who had waited patiently at the hotel with other spouses while we were at the press event, heard our complaints and with a grin remarked, "Do you know how many people in the world would have loved to be in your shoes today?" He was right. It was professionally a failure, but it was a once-in-a-lifetime experience.

I have also had my share of strange interviews. One time I was waiting for an A-list actor, who was very late. The film in which he was starring was a buddy film, and he was paired with his co-star for the roundtable. I saw the younger actor in the hallway, but there was no sign of the older actor. After about a half-hour of waiting, he finally arrived—stoned. He rambled and mumbled aimlessly during the interview. His incoherent babble combined with the glassiness of his eyes made for an uncomfortable situation. Luckily for him, his co-star managed to help him out and provide some interesting information about their experience making the film. Otherwise, the interview would have been a complete, and I mean complete, zero. Who was this actor? Let's just say that he had a successful TV show in the 1980s and went on to have a lucrative career as an action film star.

Another interview was not as much strange as it was demanding. The first time I interviewed Robin Williams, I roared with laughter. He interspersed one-liners with his answers and also did some sidesplitting impersonations. It was truly delightful. But when it came time to transcribe my interview with him, I cursed his name. The man talks a mile a minute! Fortunately, what he has to say is not only funny, but also worth reporting. But if it weren't for the slow-motion playback on my tape recorder, I don't know if the feature article would have materialized.

A third interview was strange but also completely entertaining. While some of my colleagues look down on this type of interview, it was perfect for the publication that assigned the story. *The Princess and the Frog,* Disney's animated film that introduced Princess Tiana, was about to be released on DVD and Blu-ray. My job was to interview Princess Tiana. No, I was not supposed to interview Anika Noni-Rose, the actress that provided the voice of Tiana in the film. I was to interview Princess Tiana, herself. How, you might wonder, could anyone interview an animated character? I submitted a list of questions for Tiana to the studio, and the filmmakers answered them the way the character would. Because this was for a family publication, I enlisted two young girls to help me with the questions. They adored the film (and Tiana) and supplied me with plenty of things they wanted to know about her. I learned that Tiana's favorite foods were okra casserole and bananas foster. I also learned that, besides cooking, she liked to read. When I asked her to give advice to young girls who looked up to Disney princesses, she said, "Dream as big as you can, then work hard to make those dreams come true." This was definitely an unconventional interview, but in this business there is really no such thing as a normal interview.

Interviews can be strange, not just because of the things actors say, but also because of the things they don't say. The Television Critics Association Press Tours are held twice a year for networks to introduce their new shows and to revisit some of their hit shows. Getting into the TCA is difficult, even for seasoned journalists.

We must apply for membership, which has standards. No tabloid journalists are allowed. As a result, the questions journalists ask of the members of the panels are professional and well thought out. But once in a while, we do find ourselves with nothing to ask. One time, we experienced an uncomfortable silence during one of the panels for a new series. Usually during the panels there are plenty of questions for the actors and showrunners, but this time, a silence fell over the ballroom. We could all tell that the show was not going to be successful, and we felt there was really nothing very interesting to discuss with the cast. The network reps asked if there were any more questions, and no one raised a hand. Then, out of sheer desperation, one of the stars, Mimi Rogers, mentioned that she was once married to Tom Cruise. She was hoping to get a dialogue going, but instead an uncomfortable silence followed. Awkward!

Sometimes, the format of the interview can bring strange or less-than-desirable results. There are several types of interviews. Journalists vie for the one-on-one interview, where actors and journalists meet face to face. In this situation, journalists can get exclusive comments and ask questions that are specific to their particular assignment or publication.

Roundtables are less desirable than face-to-face interviews, but still second best. In this situation, the talent (actor, filmmaker, etc.) is brought into a room with a round table. There, he or she sits with a group of journalists, answers questions, and then moves on to another room with another group of journalists. I have been in roundtables with anywhere from three to twenty journalists. The smaller the better. That gives each of us more time for our own questions.

The press conference format is what most studios are offering these days. I have never quite figured out why they went to this format. Perhaps it is because of finances. Instead of securing several different rooms for roundtables, they only need to secure one banquet room. This way the talent needs only to appear one time. The problem with this is that everyone, and I do mean everyone, gets the same quotes. You can read the same statement in a magazine, an East Coast newspaper, a mid-Atlantic newspaper, a Southern newspaper, a Western newspaper, and sometimes even a foreign newspaper. This makes our job seem less impressive. When everyone has the exact same quote from Matt Damon, why would readers want to purchase a different magazine or go to a new website when there is nothing new?

Then there are the phoners. Phone interviews can be done either as one-to-one interviews or as conferences. For me, they are preferable to the massive press conferences; however, phone conferences don't provide critical information to journalists, such as facial expressions or the interviewee's appearance. Sometimes mannerisms and expressions are worth writing about.

Despite the lack of visual information, phoners definitely come in handy. One time, I had a phone interview with Madonna when she was back East and I was in Los Angeles. It was the only way to interview her. She was in NYC for a short time, and I needed to talk to her about her latest project. The phoner sure beat traveling five or six hours on a plane for a twenty-minute interview, then enduring a return flight. I also enjoyed phoning Patty Duke instead of traveling to her home in Idaho. When a face-to-face interview is impossible, a phone interview is a great way to get some first-hand information for an article.

In an effort to avoid the strange or meaningless interviews, some journalists refuse to participate in phone conferences. Others will not take part in press conferences and insist upon one-on-one interviews (when they can get them). But most of the time, we take what we can get.

When I asked my colleagues, "What is the strangest interview you have ever conducted?" I got some pretty interesting answers. I think you will be surprised by what they said.

Howard Benjamin, Interview Factory Radio Networks

First of all, I have conducted over 50,000 interviews over the course of my career, so picking one is really tough. There was the time I showed up at a hotel to interview "The Godfather of Soul," Mr. James Brown; and, as I got to the door of his suite, I heard him on the phone, in a raised voice, demanding that he be paid $20,000 for his performance the night before. It seems that his wages were garnished by the Marshals as a part of a bankruptcy judgment. He angrily answered the door and told me to come back later. When I returned, the interview became a nightmare, and he put me through a living hell. About a year later, a publicist I trusted called to offer, who else, James Brown. I told him "no thanks," and he said, "Please do it for me." I finally said yes, and upon entering the publicist's office, I was greeted by the "Godfather" himself. With open arms, he motioned for me to come forward as he wanted to hug me. As I approached he said, "I put you through hell, didn't I?" My answer was, "I've been to hell, and it was a picnic compared to my last experience with you." We both laughed, and he apologized.

After that interview, he asked me to come back that night to interview him on camera for an HBO special about his life. I asked, "Why would you choose me? There must be a thousand African-American journalists that would love to have this opportunity." He said, "It's because they grew up with me being a fixture in their musical lives; you, on the other hand, took the time to find out everything that you could so that my story would be told right." We became lifelong friends from that day forward.

Another strange experience was the day I was asked to interview Academy Award winner Lee Marvin. HBO was scheduled to broadcast a welcome-home celebration for Vietnam veterans from Washington, D.C. on the 4th of July, 1986, and they wanted Mr. Marvin to read a few public service announcements for the upcoming concert. He was given all the proper information concerning the event; but, when I arrived to record the spots and do the interview, he pretended that he was unaware and refused to do it. I am a Vietnam veteran, and I began to try and change his mind. He agreed to do the interview but would have nothing to do with reading the HBO concert material.

At one point in the interview, he informed me that he was one of the foremost experts on Post-Traumatic Stress as it relates to Vietnam veterans, and I asked how long he had studied the syndrome. He remarked that he had spent two weeks in Vietnam, and that's why he was so well-versed in the disorder. He saw that I was less than impressed with his credentials. He became more agitated as time went on, and to be quite frank, he began to argue every question I asked in my interview. I am a man of extreme patience, but enough was enough, and I finally said, "If you don't like the questions I'm asking you, let's switch the subject to a word that you helped find its way into the English lexicon: palimony!" He went crazy. (It was his separation from his common-law wife, Michelle Triola Marvin, and her quest for financial compensation that modified the term "alimony" for a spouse to "palimony" for an unmarried couple.)

It seems I had finally got to him the way he had been toying with me, and he began to stand up in a very confrontational manner. I said, "I've had enough of your ill-tempered attitude," and asked him to step outside so we could settle the matter. He sat back down and eventually read the HBO copy. I guess I had made my point in a manner he could accept. There are so many more situations I could relate, but let those serve as the good and the bad. I'll leave the ugly for another time.

Rick Bentley, *Fresno Bee*

For the 50th anniversary of *Snow White and the Seven Dwarfs*, I was invited to talk to Snow White. I assumed this would either be the original voice—Adriana Caselotti—or someone who plays Snow White in one of the Disney parks. It was neither. I was to interview Snow White as if she were a living, breathing person. After a few questions about living in the woods with seven men, there was nothing left about which we could talk.

Mike Reynolds, Veteran Entertainment Journalist

At the time of this incident, this female music performer was embarking on her career and was unknown but went on to become very famous. The interview was conducted in a large boardroom with only the two of us present. Fairly quickly into the interview, she got up onto the table and began answering questions while prowling around on all fours in a very sexy manner. It got more intense as the interview continued and became very embarrassing. She seemed more intent on trying to elicit some physical response than on answering questions. With all the movement and a lavalier microphone attached to her clothing, the interview was barely usable because of all the rustling against the mic. Knowing I didn't have such a fatal attraction toward the opposite sex was further confirmed later when another journalist recounted his similar experience in interviewing her in that same room.

Another time was with a female actor, who was very famous at the time. Two chairs facing one another had been placed in a room. The actress took her seat on one and I began to prepare my recording equipment. I had my lavalier microphone and somehow found myself behind her, slightly puzzled at where I was going to put it. The actress was wearing a low-cut dress looking as if it had been painted onto her curvaceous body—it was so tight! The dress was not only low at the top but high at the bottom, exposing plenty of leg.

Sensing my predicament, the actress grabbed the top of her dress with both hands and pulled the top away from her. I could see everything! "Put it here," she suggested. What could I do? It was an invitation I had to accept. That over, I connected the microphone to the machine, pulled out my notes, and sat down opposite her. She was very good and extremely friendly. However, when the interview began she sat demurely (as best she could in such a dress), with her legs together—but as the interview continued, her legs moved further and further apart. We were sitting far enough away from one another that after a while, when looking down at my notes to check on something, I couldn't help but notice that the actress was not wearing underwear! With that, I just had to bring the notebook further up so my eyes didn't return south. Well, that's my version, anyway!

Another time was with another music performer. While I had interviewed this performer previously, he was now better known than ever. I went to his hotel room and knocked on the door. When it opened, I was greeted by a room in darkness, save for a few candles positioned around the room. It was a hot mid-afternoon in Los Angeles! It was explained to me that he was in some form of meditation demanding this ambiance and couldn't put lights on until much later on. Try working recording equipment under those conditions. Needless to say, the interview was less than stellar, and there was much rambling about the newfound "religion."

George Pennacchio, KABC-TV

I think it's when I interview animated characters. Movie studios sometimes set up special rooms where we can ask questions of Rugrats, characters from *The Incredibles,* or a penguin from *Mr. Popper's Penguins.* Their answers are preproduced, and you use the Q&A to create a fun, silly piece. It's just different.

Donna Plesh, Thecolumnists.com

I don't know if it would be considered "strange," but I had a phone interview scheduled with an actor in a Top 10 TV series. Anyway, when I was finally able to contact the actor—well, it was the worst interview ever. He gave me one-word answers to my questions—"Yes" or "No." So there really was no interview. A waste of his time and my time. Definitely the worst interview ever.

Dave Walker, *New Orleans Times-Picayune*

It was one of the "Swamp People." I didn't understand a word. I never wrote the article.

Brian Sebastian, Movie Reviews & More

First off the top of my head is John Goodman. He was promoting four movies, and we had him for a limited time for radio due to his schedule. *The Borrowers, Big Lebowski, Fallen,* and *Matinee,* and he had nothing to say. Nothing! How do you have four movies coming out and nothing to say about them? He was scared of the mics. That's when I figured out that certain celebrities are better for TV and not radio.

Bonnie Siegler, Freelance

I had to wait two and a half hours in the bowels of the old *Los Angeles Herald* newspaper building downtown in 100+ degree weather for Peter Weller. I don't know if this is strange or not, but when he did give me some time, he was chowing down on a bag of popcorn, giving one-syllable answers, and left after ten minutes.

Sean Daly, *New York Post*

I interviewed a band in a bathroom stall at the ROXY on Sunset Boulevard once. Does that count? One of the most memorable interviews happened at a movie junket with Tara Reid in about 2003. She walked into a small roundtable—maybe three journalists—and as she sat down, her publicist made the huge mistake of showing her an article in a magazine that just came out that quoted Tara saying, "I am still in love with Carson Daly." Well, she absolutely freaked out! Started crying, shaking . . . Someone asked her a question about the movie, and she ended up having a complete meltdown: "Why does everybody hate me?"

I was also sitting with Drew Barrymore in a hotel room doing an interview when she burst into tears. I turned around and realized she was looking at the TV over my shoulder. It was a few weeks after 9/11, and the U.S. had just gone to war.

Alex Strachan, *Postmedia News*

In strictly entertainment terms, it would have to be a camera operator on the set of a shoot in a Vancouver sci-fi show, just moments after the star of the show—who shall go unnamed—lost his temper at this guy and reamed him out in front of the director and full crew.

Jacqueline Cutler, Tribune Media Services

Farrah Fawcett. The interview stretched over many hours, and she kept calling me back. Six times in one day. She called from the bath at one point as I heard splashing and asked where she was. Later she called and was driving. She sounded disoriented, and I asked her to pull over and just sit there. It was a very odd interview.

Stephen Whitty, *Star-Ledger*

During a phone interview, Pia Zadora told me she was a little crazy because she was having her period, then kept interrupting our chat to yell at her maid and threaten to have her deported. That was odd. Tiny Tim sang AC/DC's "Highway to Hell" for me. That was peculiar. Terrence Howard greeted me in his hotel room in his pajamas, played me several of his own songs on the guitar, and frequently wiped away tears. I still have no idea what was going on that day.

Michael Lee, RadioFree.com

I'm sure there are other examples, but the strangest interview that immediately pops to mind is more a situation of venue rather than interview subject, and it's not even related to the film world. It was around the time of the 2004 Olympics. I was doing some sports coverage and attended a WNBA game at the Staples Center in Los Angeles in the hopes of interviewing players from various national teams. Whereas most interviews are coordinated affairs with press check-ins and a publicist to wrangle you in the right direction, this was almost uncomfortably informal. It was basically, "The players should be done dressing. Go in the locker room and find whoever you want to interview." A guy barging into a women's locker room seems strange enough, but the added pressure of speaking to only the subjects of interest (and the implication that you'd like to exclude the rest of the team) seemed particularly awkward. The players were also in the midst of getting ready, so it seemed somehow invasive to interrupt whatever pre-game rituals they might have with media questions.

Candace Havens, FYI Television

There are different kinds of strange, so this question is hard. I once had to interview a singer during a NASCAR race, while the cars were racing by. We couldn't move somewhere quieter because something was wrong with security. It worked, but it wasn't easy.

Julio Martinez, *VIP Latino Magazine*, KPFK Radio

I interviewed Mickey Rooney while he was naked in his dressing room.

David Sheehan, Hollywood Close-Ups, Inc.

That would be Marlon Brando when he threw a paper coffee cup at me in jest because he thought I was trying to go along with his agenda.

Scott Pierce, *Salt Lake Tribune*

In terms of setting, it would have to be the time that Rob Owen of the *Pittsburgh Post-Gazette* and I were extras on the sci-fi series *Crusade* (a spinoff of *Babylon 5*). We interviewed creator/

executive producer J. Michael Straczynski in his office while we were still wearing the uniforms we'd been given for our parts as extras. I also once did a call with a rather big movie/TV actress who was clearly, um, impaired.

Fred Topel, Crave Online

I was in a roundtable interview with Joaquin Phoenix while they were filming *I'm Still Here*. The thing is, everybody already thought it was a hoax, and he was trying to convince us he was seriously becoming a rapper. And Casey Affleck was filming it and asking all of us why we didn't take it seriously! So I think it was a flawed premise at the early stages.

Rob Salem, *Toronto Star*

That would have to be Michael Richards in a stairwell at the 1995 Cannes Festival.

Winnie Bonelli, North Jersey Media Group

Probably the strangest was interviewing Dr. Dre, who decided to have his car detailed with me as his captive passenger. Some two and a half hours later, we got back to his apartment and my car.

Valerie Milano, *Hollywood Today*

Jersey Shore's Deena Nicole Cortese. I was slightly distracted by her glow-in-the-dark contact lenses—her eyes looked more than slightly tiger-ish.

Hanh Nguyen, TVGuide.com

I interviewed the conlanger David J. Peterson about creating the Dothraki language for HBO's *Game of Thrones*. He taught me to curse in Dothraki, which probably isn't wise since I'd be quickly julienned if I were to be so lippy with those nomadic warriors.

Margie Barron, *Production Update*

The strangest interview? The Olsen twins were toddlers, on stage by themselves, and in front of a roomful of reporters. You could see they were scared and didn't know what to say when the reporters started firing questions at them both at the same time. I tried to make them more at ease by asking Mary Kate a question, and then asking Ashley a question. Still, it was painful to see the scared looks on their faces.

Aaron Barnhart, *Kansas City Star*

I interviewed Elvis Costello about his hosting gig for a Sundance Channel talk show, and it just never got on track. And then at the end, after I had gotten almost nothing out of him, we got to talking about Charlie Parker, who had grown up in Kansas City, and the fact he had made an LP with a string orchestra. Elvis said, "Oh, if you like that, you should get *Clifford Brown with Strings.*" I did, and it is one of my favorite jazz records ever. And every time I play it, I think of Elvis.

5

Twilight Zone Moments

Every once in a while, journalists walk out of a room and wonder exactly what happened in there. I call these "Twilight Zone moments." You know those times when someone is talking, and you cannot figure out how they got from point A to point B? Perhaps they misunderstood the question, or perhaps they simply wanted to digress onto another topic, but the fact remains that they said something completely unexpected. The Romans called it a "non sequitur." We call it "out there."

A good example of a Twilight Zone moment occurred at the 2010 Television Critics Association Press Tour when Yoko Ono came to discuss the PBS documentary, *Lennon NYC*. This film depicts the years John Lennon spent in New York with Yoko and their son, Sean. John is depicted in the film as a regular guy in New York (as if John Lennon could be a regular guy anywhere). The couple took walks in the park and ate at the local restaurants. Then John decided to record a new album with his wife. Shortly thereafter, on December 8, 1980, Lennon was tragically shot outside of his Dakota apartment building with his wife at his side.

At the TCA press conference, a colleague of mine asked Yoko why she decided to stay in New York, and specifically at The

Dakota, after her husband was killed. Every time she walked on the path outside of her apartment, she stepped on the very place her husband was shot. It was a legitimate question. After all, Jacqueline Kennedy had stated that she would never go back to Dallas because of the horrific memories of the day her husband was killed.

Yoko Ono became angry with the question, claiming it was racist and sexist. She went on and on about how sexist it was. "No one would have asked it if I had been a man," she stated. We were astonished at her behavior, and I personally couldn't understand her reaction. I kept replaying it in my mind as I drove home later that evening.

When the official transcript of the session arrived from PBS, I was eager to read it. I thought perhaps I had been mistaken about Yoko's reaction. But the transcript, quoted below, confirmed that my astonishment was justified. Keep in mind that English is not Ms. Ono's first language.

> **YOKO ONO:** I think people say, "Why are you still living on Dakota?" You know, I think it is a slightly racist remark, and maybe sexist, too, because I'm sure that many people are living in their own house, own house, own home, that he or she shared with their spouses, even after the spouse has passed away, especially because they passed away, because there's a lot of memory, and also you built the place with the spouse. I'm not going to leave that and go to some strange house that I never went to. This is something we built, and when you go inside, you see that each room is something that we made it well, maybe it for us."

A reasonable statement, to be sure. But then she was asked a different question.

> **QUESTION:** What would John think about the Internet, Facebook, and Twitter?

YOKO ONO: Wait a second. I want to answer more fully about what he said, because that's sexist and racist. The thing is, you guys are doing that, but when somebody like me, who is probably not part of your culture, how you think, "Why she still living there? We wouldn't live there. Well, maybe because she has a different tradition and she doesn't care about the fact that he died there." You know, something like that. A little bit more barbaric or something. No. I think that you would want to live there, too, because you have—you cherish the memory of that person. That's one. So that's—but also the other thing is, for you to be able to say something like that, "How dare she's living there?" is sexism, because I know that all guys wouldn't care. They would just live in the house, you know, whatever happens. They may not even care that they got a divorce or whatever happened. They would just live in the house, and no one's going to comment. No one's going to comment that you would go to maybe a whorehouse or something like that right after your wife died. "I'm so sorry. He must be so sad." (Laughter.) I was still sad, so I'm still living in that house. Do you mind?

QUESTION: Listen. I'm sorry. Okay. I did not mean to be racist or sexist, and I don't know how whorehouses got into this conversation.

YOKO ONO: You know what I'm talking about. If it's a guy, they're not going to comment.

QUESTION: When my dad passed away, my mom wanted to go live in Florida, and it's just people grieve differently. All I was really asking you was you could have walked away. Maybe it was too painful to live there. Some people grieve one way. Some people grieve another. But New York obviously means a great deal to you.

YOKO ONO: Means so much to us and so much to me now, especially because John was there, is with me.

Other Twilight Zone moments occur when people purposely don't answer a question. You see this with politicians all the time. They never really get to the point. This happens with celebrities as well, although not as regularly as it does with politicians. For example, during the interview for the film, *You, Me and Dupree*, Matt Dillon was asked about the offers he had received since his role in *Crash*. He responded: "Generally, I like to do comedy; but I'll be perfectly honest, I like to do drama and more character-driven-based stuff. But I like to do comedy, and I found this is one of the more difficult roles that I've had to play recently—because the character's the straight guy, he's very reactive." What kind of roles had he been offered? I don't know. He never answered the question. Those are the times we ask follow-up questions, trying to get a satisfactory answer, but we're not always successful. That's just the nature of the beast.

Sometimes, in an effort to avoid answering a question, a celebrity will start talking about something unrelated, like the set of his or her upcoming movie or a meaningful experience from childhood. Sometimes these are interesting stories that make for good articles, but many times they are simply red herrings designed to redirect questions.

For this chapter, my colleagues were asked, "Have you ever had a Twilight Zone moment?" As you are about to find out, celebrities are not always at their best while being interviewed.

George Pennacchio, KABC-TV

Yes! While I won't name names, I will say I'm guessing drugs were involved. And not by me!

Michael Lee, RadioFree.com

I don't know if I've ever had a Twilight Zone moment per se, but there are rare occasions of talent giving bluntly honest answers, which is only memorable because we're accustomed to diplomatic responses.

Scott Pierce, *Salt Lake Tribune*

Well, there was the *Kingdom Hospital* press conference, when Diane Ladd started talking about her actual encounters with ghosts. Not the fictional ghosts in the miniseries. Actual ghosts.

Candace Havens, FYI Television

I'm going to lie and say no, that has never happened. My favorites are the executive producers with the doublespeak. You ask why they let a certain star go, and they tell you all of this stuff about how the show is moving in a new direction. Then some janitor on the set tells you it was because she never showed up at work on time, and she screamed at her co-workers.

Howard Benjamin, Interview Factory Radio Networks

When you watch Barbara Walters interview one of her guests, there is always that moment when she makes them cry. Well, recently I was speaking to a new artist, and we were about half an hour into our conversation when I brought up a specific song he had written. It was about a failed relationship; and, before I could ask him if it was a true life experience, he began to openly weep—so much so that he found it difficult to continue. It took ten minutes for him to regain his composure. That ten minutes came out of the interview time. If he becomes as big a star as I think he will, it's ten minutes that I could have asked him many more questions.

Along the same lines, I used to ask a question when some kind of sixth sense I have kicked in about whether the interview subject had ever experienced a near-death accident. I got that feeling while talking to country music star Patty Loveless. She stopped for a second and then began to relay the story of how she almost drowned while visiting her older sister when she was in her early teens. It had such a profound impact on her life that she really never got over the trauma to this day. It also stopped the interview cold while she went through the emotional déjà vu.

Mike Reynolds, Veteran Entertainment Journalist

Too many to recall one over and above the rest. There are too many strange people out there—even (especially) amongst celebrities.

Valerie Milano, *Hollywood Today*

I probably had too much to drink, but I didn't remember a word that Oliver Platt said in his drunken stupor when he was in *Huff* in 2004. Those TCA parties—whew . . .

Rob Owen, *Pittsburgh Post-Gazette*

Yes. It was back when UPN still existed. So, UPN's on TV and *Star Trek Voyager* is one of their shows. UPN on their TCA Press Tour day had some round robins. They had the actors move from table to table, and I was at a table. Kate Mulgrew, who played Captain Janeway, sits down, and somebody asks her, "What do you think should happen for the cliffhanger at the end of this season?" At the time, her contract was up, and she was in negotiations. She said, "Well, I think they should kill off Janeway." And so everybody leans in a little closer. "What is it you think they should do?" "I think they should kill off Janeway. I think it would be great for the show if they killed off Janeway." So then we ran to, I believe it was Paul McGuire, who was in charge of UPN publicity at the time, and said, "Kate Mulgrew thinks they should kill off Janeway. Does the network have any comment on this?" Within a few hours, Kate Mulgrew was calling all of the critics who had been at that particular table to clarify her comments and make it clear that she did not want to leave the show. So her attempt to negotiate through the press, I suspect, ended with a strong reprimand from the network.

Julio Martinez, *VIP Latino Magazine*, KPFK Radio

I interviewed David and Keith Carradine together when they had a band that was playing at the Wilshire Ebell. Keith was answering a question of mine when David just started talking some stream-of-consciousness jabber, stood up, and talked himself right out of the room. Keith watched him leave and then said, "I'd better help him with that," and walked off after him. This did give me the opportunity to talk to their father, John Carradine, who was a lot more interesting, anyway.

Hanh Nguyen, TVGuide.com

I was in a roundtable interview with three other journalists and talking to Kirsten Dunst about *Elizabethtown* in 2005. I asked her about the upcoming *Spider-Man 3* film's villains, which had not been officially announced. These were the days when movie scoops were not really that closely guarded; so, after telling me that Topher Grace and Thomas Haden Church were cast as Venom and Sandman, she turned to her publicist and said, "That's out, right?" It was not.

I felt like a shoplifter trying to look cool while leaving that interview. I quickly and quietly wrote the story and was the first to post it. Unfortunately, since it was a roundtable interview, I could not use the word "exclusive." MTV picked up the story and used the phrasing "told reporters," and thus it became everybody's story.

Later, at another press day for *Tristan and Isolde*, James Franco told reporters who were at a separate roundtable from mine that he could not discuss *Spider-Man 3* at all since Dunst had gotten into trouble for spilling the casting news. Those reporters came up to me later, half-joking, half-congratulatory: "Dammit, Hanh! You ruined it for us."

Sean Daly, *New York Post*

I interviewed Ozzy Osbourne in 2001. I spent almost an hour with him talking about everything imaginable—drugs, his family, rock and roll . . . It was only after I left that the next journalist on her way in asked me, "Did he talk about the reality show?" Reality show? What reality show? A few months later, *The Osbournes* was the biggest TV hit of the year.

Jacqueline Cutler, Tribune Media Services

This was before I was officially covering entertainment, but one of the oddest had to be in June 1980. Henry Miller had just died, and a memorial service was held for him at Plato's Retreat, a sex club. I had been working as a reporter already but had graduated college a couple of weeks before. Al Goldstein, the publisher of *Screw Magazine*, was following me around, wearing a very detailed, very large gold chain of a naked woman and saying nasty things to me. I had dressed in the 1980 equivalent of a hippie burka and just kept trying to interview people, but afterward I remember standing in the street, trying to process everything he and others had said to me.

Stephen Whitty, *Star-Ledger*

Sometimes things just are odd from the beginning. Sometimes they take a wrong turn. Morgan Freeman got oddly defensive and combative for reasons I still don't quite understand—I wonder if he misheard or misunderstood a question. Tommy Lee Jones—who is a famously bad interview—was fine with me at first. Then he ordered his second drink and started flirting with a lady across the bar. It was like pulling teeth after that. Sometimes things just go south, and if you only have half an hour or so with someone, it can be hard to recover in time.

Winnie Bonelli, North Jersey Media Group

Probably the moment after I interviewed Robin Williams. He was hilarious, told jokes galore, jumped around the room, talked to his penis. Only afterwards did I realize there wasn't one thing I could write for a family newspaper.

Brian Sebastian, Movie Reviews & More

You mention "Twilight Zone," and Bruce Dern and Nick Nolte come to mind. Ask them one question, and you're gonna get a long answer to nothing. Oh, and by the way, Bruce Dern holds the record in the radio room for longest answer—41 minutes—and it had nothing to do with the movie!

Rob Salem, *Toronto Star*

Not sure what you mean there, but I did have a *"Star Trek"* moment. Actually, several—I have been on every *Trek* set except the first.

But it was right after the roundtable session on the junket for I think *Star Trek IV* or *Star Trek V*. I got on the elevator, and then Shatner and Nimoy walked in. Now, I am a long-time Trekkie geek, but I have endeavored to keep my professional cool every time I encounter these icons of my youth.

I thought I was betraying no outward emotion, though there was an excited 12-year-old leaping up and down inside me, saying, "I'm on the turbo-lift with Kirk and Spock! I'm on the turbo-lift with Kirk and Spock!"

Since I'm standing in front of the button panel, I ask them which floor. Shatner looks at me, then at Nimoy, then back at me. "Bridge," he says. Busted.

Alex Strachan, *Postmedia News*

Not really—nothing really surprises me, anymore. And I find most people who work in the entertainment field have been around enough and are savvy enough to know that, even when they're pretending to speak their mind and say something really dumb, it's all calculated. Some of the dumbest, strangest things I've heard people say come up in group press conference situations, like TCA, and not in one-on-ones. One-on-ones always make better interviews, but it's also true that the talent tends to be more guarded of what they say or how they come across. That's been my experience, anyway. I'm sure I've had more than a few Twilight Zone moments, but none spring to mind.

Tim Riley, *Woodland Daily Democrat*

I have had casual conversations with celebrities at press tour parties and have often wondered why I wasted my time.

6

The Elusive Interview

Interviews with celebrities, especially A-listers, can be difficult to secure. But most of the time, it is not the celebrity who is to blame—it's the publicist. Publicists run Hollywood, and navigating this network of gatekeepers is a daunting but essential task of entertainment journalists.

When studios put on press junkets (whether they be roundtables, press conferences, one-on-ones, or social settings), there are many publicists who come into play. The studio publicists send out invitations to individual journalists, but oftentimes these publicists don't have the final say on the list of attendees. On one occasion, I was invited by a studio to attend a roundtable junket for the 2003 film *Mona Lisa Smile* that was about to be released. The star of the film was Julia Roberts. After I accepted the invitation, I was then "uninvited."

How did this happen? Oftentimes, studios will compile a list of journalists and forward the list to the actors' personal publicists. This happens especially if the stars are A-listers. For some reason, the publicist of this particular celebrity did not approve me in the final list of journalists. I have no idea why. I had never written anything against the actress; in fact, I had never written anything about her, period. But that's the way it is, and unfortunately, it is quite common. Some things in this business just don't have any rhyme or reason, and being uninvited from a junket is one of them.

A few years ago, I attended another roundtable junket for *Shrek 2*, a film with an impressive cast of celebrities. After the first couple of celebrities came and went, one of the journalists at the table left the room. Then in came one of the stars for her portion of the junket. When she left the room, the journalist returned. He explained that he was allowed to take part in the junket but could not stay for this particular actress's portion. Her publicist would not allow him in the room when she was there, because he worked for a tabloid newspaper.

In addition to choosing *which* journalists are allowed to participate in press junkets, publicists also manage *when* journalists are allowed to speak with their clients. Publicists do not want people to interview their clients unless they are promoting something, like a book, movie, CD, DVD, product, or event. This hit home to me when my editor assigned me to write a story about Michael J. Fox. The task was to tell a story about how his career progressed throughout his life and how he and his wife (also an actress) balanced their family life together with their separate professional lives. I spoke to the actor's publicist at length about my assignment but was told that the actor was not promoting anything, so he would not be able to participate. The actor lost out on a nice article and a lot of free publicity because his publicist declined the interview.

Publicists also determine which publications they will allow their actors to be interviewed by. Often, they will ask the readership or circulation (for print publications) before considering whether or not to grant interviews with their clients. At the Television Critics Association Press Tour, I often request one-on-ones, and I am approved for about half of those I request. Time is often at a premium, and if an actor is heavily booked, then the publicist prefers to grant interviews to the larger publications. More bang for the buck.

Actors do figure into the decision-making process to some extent. Some celebrities simply don't do interviews or restrict their interviews to certain outlets. For example, Adam Sandler rarely does interviews for print publications. Other actors, particularly after public incidents like a divorce or drug arrest, sometimes limit their exposure to journalists until the furor dies down—even though they are supposed to promote their latest film or TV show. For the 2005 film, *Rumor Has It,* Jennifer Aniston was paired with Shirley MacLaine for the roundtables. Ms. MacLaine was very protective of Aniston, who was going through a public divorce from Brad Pitt at the time. MacLaine stated,

> [Jennifer] has come through what must be one of the most painful and difficult requirements of any human being, much less a young person: to live their life in a spotlight like this is so painful. And to have to work and do three pictures a year? That's really hard to separate your sense of whatever you're going through inside—growing up, I might add. And I'm really proud of her for the way she is handling this. . . . Her emotional discipline is extraordinary, and I really want to compliment her for that.

Aniston was presented with Ms. MacLaine because of her situation, and the publicists were doing what they could to shield her from unwanted personal questions. At least Jennifer Aniston had the class to show up for the junket. Others have simply refused to attend in these kinds of situations.

In short, publicists are the head honchos. If you think the actors are in charge, think again. The publicists reign supreme. If they don't like you, then you are out! If they want something from you, then you are wooed. If you are just starting out, you have to continually keep in touch with them so they will learn your name.

For this chapter, journalists were asked, "Is there anyone you have not been able to interview, even though you have tried?" The common theme is that interviews commonly fall apart, and we learn to appreciate what we can get.

Howard Benjamin, Interview Factory Radio Networks

How much time do you have? Bruce Springsteen comes to mind, as does Rod Stewart. There have to be hundreds of artists that I was all set to interview when it all fell apart, and in most of those cases they never were rescheduled.

George Pennacchio, KABC-TV

Elizabeth Taylor's old publicist used to tell me she watched me all the time, but I could never get a commitment for her to sit down with me. It'd also be great to have a nice chat with Doris Day—but she said goodbye to Hollywood a long time ago. As a cub entertainment reporter, I got all of one sentence from her at The Monterey Film Festival back in the '80s. I will probably have to be satisfied with that one fleeting moment. However, I'd like to think she'd like talking to me because she's a real animal lover, and my wife and I rescue greyhounds.

David Sheehan, Hollywood Close-Ups, Inc.

Not really—although I must say I never did get as much time with Jack Nicholson as I would have liked, and now he's not doing interviews at all.

Hanh Nguyen, TVGuide.com

Tina. Effin. Fey! I think it's because they know we'd be instant BFFs and then neither of us would ever get any work done. Or maybe she's just too good for me.

Mike Reynolds, Veteran Entertainment Journalist

A certain TV star has been brought to me for interviews on many occasions, but he always has his manager tailing him. I only do one-on-one interviews, and that means one person talking to one other person, not anyone else listening or watching in the same room. This manager refuses to leave; and, while I explain that I have interviewed royalty and U.S. presidents and had Secret Service agents and security leave the room for those interviews, this manager refuses to move, so I don't do the interview. It might sound like a diva-ish request, but my job is to get the best interview possible—and the only way to do that is to have an intimate conversation. That way, it's 100% attention for and from each person. As soon as one other person is invited into the mix, you are down to 50% attention. Should that "interloper" cough, laugh, or make any other noise during a great answer, you are never going to get the interviewee to repeat the full story in the same way. And, of course, it disturbs the flow of the conversation.

Rob Owen, *Pittsburgh Post-Gazette*

Jason Kilar, the founder of Hulu, grew up in Pittsburgh. Getting an interview with him is a nut I have not been able to crack.

Meg Mimura, *Lighthouse*

Too many to list. Melina Kanakaredes and Chandra Wilson come to mind. It took me several years to prove that mine is a legitimate magazine. It's still a niche of a niche, though. So I don't blame publicists who don't even return my calls, but I just move on. I either take action or find somebody else, although I did go down to Austin, Texas, to chat with Kyle Chandler. Unfortunately, "yes" didn't seem to be in his publicist's vocabulary.

Rick Bentley, *Fresno Bee*

I have a realistic attitude when it comes to celebrity interviews. There's no reason to go after some celebrities who have reached such a high point in their careers that they can be very selective. Getting an interview is a privilege and not a right.

The best thing is to be appreciative when any interview comes along. You never know when some third-stringer on a TV show will become a huge star.

Julio Martinez, *VIP Latino Magazine*, KPFK Radio

Yes. Shirley Temple (Black) in 1989. It was just after her autobiography came out. She danced with my father in 1943 at the Hollywood canteen. At first, her rep said she would be happy to talk to me, and then her schedule changed.

Sean Daly, *New York Post*

Someone asked me this question about ten years ago. I told them that when I was in grade school in NYC, my best friend was a boy named Robert Chambers, who went on to become NYC's infamous "Preppy Murderer." So he encouraged me to get in touch with Robert—which I did. For months, I worked with his lawyers and his mother to negotiate a cover story for *People* magazine to coincide with his release from prison. I flew all the way to New York to do it, but he got out early and fled the country. He is now back in jail for drug possession. I no longer care to speak with him.

Gerri Miller, Freelance

I never met any of the Beatles.

Stephen Whitty, *Star-Ledger*

Most of the people who don't do a lot of interviews—Tom Cruise, Julia Roberts, Jennifer Aniston and, for some reason, a whole bunch of comedians, like Adam Sandler and Mike Myers— are people I'm not terribly interested in interviewing to begin with. But I always ask, anyway.

Sometimes, too, the people I want to interview, and who

regularly say no, will sometimes say yes, either because of the project or, more rarely, a relationship you've established.

Al Pacino, Jodie Foster, Robert Redford, and Robert De Niro don't do a lot of press, but they eventually said yes to me partly because the movies they were doing at that time needed the help. Catherine Keener is, I think, a terrific actress but someone who always refuses to talk about herself—but after interviewing her about half a dozen times about other people, she finally agreed to a profile.

Jacqueline Cutler, Tribune Media Services

Springsteen, Jeter. (Yes, I am a New Yorker living in Jersey.)

Michael Lee, RadioFree.com

I'm sure most reporters would name a celebrity who is labeled a Hollywood "A-lister" and protected by an army of publicists, handlers, and enablers. But I've always put more value on talent whose work has meant something to me personally, and so the one actor who remains on my unofficial bucket list of personalities I would like to interview is Peter Cullen, who provided the voice of Optimus Prime in the live action *Transformers* films and the '80s animated series. As a kid, Prime was my childhood superhero, much as Superman or Batman or Spider-Man might have been for others. Nostalgia trumps box office receipts. Although given the success of Michael Bay's *Transformers* films, I credit Mr. Cullen with both.

Fred Topel, Crave Online

Michael J. Fox. I had a chance to go to New York for the *Back to the Future* anniversary, but the schedule would have been insane to fly there and back. Hopefully one day I'll cover one of his foundation events.

Winnie Bonelli, North Jersey Media Group

There have been a few, most recently Joe Pesci for an assignment with *New Jersey Monthly*. Often it has nothing to do with the interviewer. Sometimes it's bad timing or something going on that they don't want to discuss and are afraid you might ask.

Brian Sebastian, Movie Reviews & More

Former Vice President Al Gore for *An Inconvenient Truth*. I tried to get him for the Santa Barbara Film Fest. It didn't happen. Also Tiger Woods—I'm still trying for him!

Dave Walker, *New Orleans Times-Picayune*

Network publicity people are usually pretty good about putting me in touch with whoever I need, especially if there's a local angle to write about. And if I'm not able to make a reasonably expeditious connection while my intent is to lavish free publicity on a show, I give up pretty quickly. There's always someone else to talk to, and always another show to write about.

Alex Strachan, *Postmedia News*

Nothing specific—I've generally been lucky in landing the interviews I want. And I've had luck landing interviews with people who are media-shy or don't give interviews as a rule. For me, the toughest "gets" are more general. Landing an on-set visit in my hometown, for example, is next to impossible if the set is closed. Emails never get returned, calls are never returned in that instance. Set visits, when a show is in production, can be really tough to arrange. And, of course, it's impossible to deal with someone— often a junior flack—if they're just not cooperative. In terms of individual talent, though, I've found that if you can get to their personal publicist, state your case, let them know who you are and exactly what you're looking for, you generally get a fair hearing.

Rob Salem, *Toronto Star*

Hmm. Hard to believe, but pretty much no. Comes with working for the largest outlet in Canada (we outsell all the other major papers combined).

I have met all my heroes and liked almost all of them.

I've always wanted to sleep with Ann Margret. Does that count?

Missed Opportunities

Entertainment professionals reminisce about Old Hollywood with nostalgia. The Golden Age of Hollywood—when the studio bosses held tight reins over their stables of talent, when movies stayed in theaters for months, and when starlets could be epitomized by the word "glamour"—is long gone. Almost every journalist would love to have interviewed someone who has gone up to the pearly gates. For me, the list is long.

Jack Lemmon is first on my list. Jack Lemmon was a consummate actor. He was equally brilliant in his dramatic role of a nuclear plant supervisor in *The China Syndrome* as he was as a man masquerading as a woman in *Some Like it Hot*. His career spanned decades, and his films focused on a variety of subjects. To me, Jack was perfection on the screen. I had a phone interview with his son, Chris Lemmon, and Chris instantly became one of my favorite people. Besides talking about his own life, Chris related stories about his father, which were priceless to me.

Next on my interview wish list is the Rat Pack: Dean Martin, Frank Sinatra, Sammy Davis, Jr., Joey Bishop, and Peter Lawford. Imagine all of this talent in one room. I don't know how much solid (and quotable) information they would have provided, considering their penchant for playing around, but it sure would have been fun from an entertainment point of view.

I would have loved to interview William Holden, who starred in *Love is a Many Splendored Thing*, *Sabrina*, *Picnic*, *The Bridge on the River Kwai*, and many other notable films. Not only was he a fine actor, but he was also an early environmentalist. I am extremely interested in his wildlife endeavors, and one of these days I would like to go to Kenya to see his foundation conservancy.

Donna Reed also makes my list. She and Jimmy Stewart starred together in *It's a Wonderful Life*, and she had her own TV show from 1958–66. I recently interviewed Paul Petersen, who played Jeff Stone in *The Donna Reed Show*, about his organization, A Minor Consideration, which works on behalf of child actors. During this interview, Paul had nothing but high praise for Donna, who played his mother on the show. Paul told me, "Donna Reed cherished education. She had to work her tail off. She was cleaning houses to go to Los Angeles City College." Paul told me stories of how generous and giving Donna was to everyone in the cast and crew. Apparently, she was also brilliant. He said, "I can't imagine the kids on the Roseanne Barr show feeling the same way I do about Donna Reed thirty-five years from now. I can't imagine it." She was definitely one of the class acts of Hollywood.

Danny Thomas would have been a fun man to interview. He accomplished so much in his life. Besides being an actor, he founded the St. Jude's Children's Research Hospital in Memphis, Tennessee. He worked tirelessly on behalf of the hospital that helps children from all walks of life, even if they cannot afford medical care. Talk about a man of conscience!

Walter Cronkite also would have been an interesting man to interview. Just think about all the things he witnessed firsthand during his long career. In particular, I think about his actions on November 22, 1963, when he informed the nation that President Kennedy had died. His statement about the assassination burns in my memory from all the film clips I have seen about that day.

On the music side of the business, I think Henry Mancini and Jerry Goldsmith would have been interesting interviews. They were extremely talented songwriters. Having grown up in a musical home, I have always had a special affinity for great music. When it comes to modern composers, these two are at the top of my list. Mancini composed the theme from *Charade*, one of my all-time favorite films. Among his other compositions are *The Pink Panther*, *Moon River*, *The Days of Wine and Roses*, the love theme from *Romeo and Juliet*, and many TV theme songs like the one for *Charlie's Angels*. Goldsmith transformed television with his themes for the *Star Trek* series, *The Man from U.N.C.L.E.*, *The Waltons*, and countless others that are part of today's pop culture. Face it, no film or TV show would be the same without music, and Henry Mancini and Jerry Goldsmith composed many of the soundtracks of our lives.

My list of missed opportunities also includes Danny Kaye (a very funny man, a humanitarian, and a man who made the classic film *White Christmas* as good as it is); Cary Grant (who wouldn't want to interview Cary Grant? Come on!); Rock Hudson (he was also great at both comedy and drama, and I enjoy watching him in *Giant*, *Magnificent Obsession*, his films with Doris Day, and his TV series, *McMillan and Wife*); Richard Burton; and many others.

For this chapter, journalists were asked, "Who would you have liked to interview that is no longer alive?" After reading their responses, my list of missed opportunities has grown to include Johnny Carson, Grace Kelly, Spencer Tracy, and John Wayne. As I look at my growing list of celebrities who are no longer with us, I wonder what it would be like to interview them. I know they would be interesting interviews, but would they disappoint me as people or live up to their larger-than-life personas?

George Pennacchio, KABC-TV

That would be Lucille Ball. The reruns of *I Love Lucy* were a part of my childhood, and I just thought she was the funniest person on television. Then I discovered *The Lucy Show* and *Here's Lucy* and *Life With Lucy* and everything else she ever did. I loved her on game shows and, as a kid, I was even at the opening weekend for *Mame*. I just never had the opportunity to meet her. I used to picture myself writing a letter to her seeing if she'd like to battle me in backgammon. I wish I had. In junior high, I paid $5 to be a member of the "We Still Love Lucy Fan Club." It was a mimeographed newsletter that came periodically! I never met Lucy, but I have decided in my mind she would have loved me. And now that I've been covering show business for so long, I've met enough of her friends who've told me they think I'm right.

Donna Plesh, Thecolumnists.com

Carroll O'Connor. Most people most likely remember him from *All in The Family*, but he did many, many TV dramas before, and several after that series. I think he was a great actor.

Howard Benjamin, Interview Factory Radio Networks

Elvis comes to mind, as does John Lennon, George Harrison, Jim Morrison, and Jimi Hendrix, as well as Humphrey Bogart and Spencer Tracy. Any of the real pioneers of TV and film like Groucho Marx, Buster Keaton, Judy Garland—the list goes on and on. All are legends and all gone much too soon. To someone whose whole life is centered on who you were able to get to open up and pour their heart out, any star, big or small, that got away is a missed opportunity.

Mike Reynolds, Veteran Entertainment Journalist

I arrived in the U.S. too late to interview Elvis, but there are so many others—Charlie Chaplin and so many of the older, earlier movie and music stars.

Sean Daly, *New York Post*

What I look for in an interview is a compelling story. The person doesn't even have to be that famous. Maybe it is the guy who invented something.

Margie Barron, *Production Update*

Gone now, but I would have liked to have interviewed John Wayne and Walt Disney.

Hanh Nguyen, TVGuide.com

Oh, I would have dearly loved to interview: Alfred Hitchcock—he's a freakin' brilliant, hilarious, and bittersweet genius; Roald Dahl—he's also brilliant and hilarious; and James Stewart—he's such a lovely actor, and I'd like to hear that folksy quaver in his voice in person and be introduced to Harvey.

Jacqueline Cutler, Tribune Media Services

Isaac Singer and Dawn Powell, because they are among my favorite writers, and Isadora Duncan and Alvin Ailey, because they were brilliant dancers.

Rick Bentley, *Fresno Bee*

The list is endless. But at the top is Gary Cooper. One of my favorite movies is *High Noon* and I would have loved to talk to him about the film.

Stephen Whitty, *Star-Ledger*

Lots of people, of course, but not necessarily the ones I would have wanted to speak to when I was just a fan. I'm a huge admirer of Alfred Hitchcock, for example, but he seemed to tell the same stories over and over again. I would have loved to sit down with Stanley Kubrick or Orson Welles, though. I would have enjoyed having a long interview with Humphrey Bogart, Katharine Hepburn, or Robert Mitchum.

Rob Owen, *Pittsburgh Post-Gazette*

I did get a chance to interview Fred Rogers on several occasions. When I moved to Pittsburgh in 1998 to become the TV writer for the *Post-Gazette*, one of the things that made that feel right was that I would be covering Mister Rogers, who I'd grown up watching as a kid. And because he was a mainstay there, perhaps I didn't make as much time to cover him as maybe I should have—and when he died so unexpectedly, suddenly I regretted that I hadn't spent more time with him. But I certainly cherish the bits of time that I did get.

Michael Lee, RadioFree.com

There are two actors I regret not meeting, and they both happened to star on the classic sitcom, *Three's Company*—John Ritter and Don Knotts. I don't know why a six-year-old kid was watching *Three's Company*, but I did, and I credit that show for inspiring my love of comedy and sitcoms. I thought I would have the opportunity to interview Don Knotts in 2005 for Disney's *Chicken Little*, but he wasn't present, and as I understand it, possibly not in the best of health at that time. John Ritter had passed away in 2003, before I started working in the world of entertainment regularly, but I still consider him one of the comedy greats who brought a lot of happiness to a lot of people. I've also heard several John Ritter stories from colleagues and people who had worked with him, and the consensus is always the same: He was a generous guy who consistently put others ahead of himself and was always warm and welcoming. When you discover that someone whose work you had admired for so long also turns out to be a great person, how can you not regret never having met them?

Scott Pierce, *Salt Lake Tribune*

Jack Benny. Johnny Carson. Lucille Ball. Desi Arnaz. George Burns. Gracie Allen. Geez, I don't know how long a list to make. I'd love to talk to the TV pioneers from classic shows.

Candace Havens, *FYI Television*

I would have loved to talk to Jimmy Stewart, Cary Grant, and Grace Kelly.

Brian Sebastian, Movie Reviews & More

James Coburn. I spoke to him in the men's room during the BFCA Luncheon, and I was to do a TV interview with him for *The Man From Elysian Fields*. Two weeks before the interview, he was sick, and two weeks after the junket he passed away.

Gerri Miller, Freelance

Elizabeth Taylor, Christopher Reeve, Michael Jackson, Johnny Carson, and plenty more.

Julio Martinez, *VIP Latino Magazine*, KPFK Radio

I wish I could have talked to crime novelist Raymond Chandler. I've had a lifelong fascination with downtown Los Angeles. My father opened a restaurant downtown, and I used to walk the streets a lot. I once went on a tour of places and locations Chandler wrote about.

Fred Topel, Crave Online

I've always felt sensitive about Brandon Lee. I would have loved to meet him. I was really excited to see him become a star.

Tim Riley, *Woodland Daily Democrat*

Alfred Hitchcock, if only to ask him how he maintained a macabre view of humanity. Jean Harlow and Marilyn Monroe—I wouldn't know how to ask the question, but I wonder how they coped, or not, with their sex-symbol status.

Winnie Bonelli, North Jersey Media Group

That's easy—Elvis Presley.

Aaron Barnhart, *Kansas City Star*

Carson, Paar, and Cosell. All difficult interviews to be sure, and they earned the right not to talk to anybody, and were terribly full of themselves. But no one has ever duplicated them, and I am now at a stage of my career where I want to know what made them tick—and it's too late!

Rob Salem, *Toronto Star*

Graham Chapman, an unrepentant drunk and the only Python I've never met. Also John Belushi, though I treasure a series of emails I got from his widow, thanking me for an appreciation I wrote on the anniversary of his death.

I would have loved to meet Gilda Radner—when she was here doing *Godspell*, I saw the show like a hundred times. I now work extensively with Gilda's Club, a resource center for those living with cancer, established in her name.

Dave Walker, *New Orleans Times-Picayune*

Johnny Carson and Jim Henson. Carson's run on *The Tonight Show* ended before I started on the beat. Then he disappeared. Then he died. Henson died a few years before I started writing about TV. Both were incredibly influential characters in our culture.

Alex Strachan, *Postmedia News*

I've gotten pretty much everyone I really wanted, in the TV industry, anyway. Peter Jennings is one person I would really have liked to do an in-depth, sit-down interview with because of the hometown element and because of my personal interest in international news, in which he was a renowned expert.

8

Open Mouth, Insert Foot

We've all done it at one time or another. It just happens. Sometimes we make a comment or ask a question that doesn't come out the way we intended, no matter how much we have rehearsed. Sometimes things get messed up between our brain and our tongue, especially when we are pressed for time. Sometimes we are trying to get in as many questions as possible, so we rush them, and they are interpreted the wrong way. And sometimes we are just having a bad day. Regardless of the reason, journalists and celebrities get tongue-tied.

One time, I attended a small press conference with Richard Gere and Diane Lane for *Nights in Rodanthe*. I asked them if they had read any of Nicholas Sparks's novels. Then I asked Richard Gere if he knew how popular the Sparks books are. Brilliant, I know. He gave me the oddest look, and I think I must have turned three shades of red. What I meant to ask was if he realized this story would be a "must-see" for Nicholas Sparks's followers, as he has a large following of fans who read his books religiously and go to all of his movies. But the question got truncated as it came out of my mouth. Yes, these things do happen—even to those of us who have been doing this for years.

Another "oops" moment happened while I was interviewing Pierce Brosnan. I have interviewed this man several times and always look forward to talking with him. He is the quintessential classy interviewee. He always comes well-dressed and is a delight to talk with. This particular time he was getting over a head cold, so he arrived with a lozenge in his mouth. Before the interview began, he took out the lozenge and placed it on a piece of paper. Then I blurted, "That's your DNA." Yes, I actually said that out loud. I had to explain that I had recently heard a story about selling another celebrity's gum or something on eBay because it had his DNA on it. Thankfully for me, Brosnan was a gentleman (as usual) and waved off the stupid comment. We continued with the interview, but I was mortified. Sometimes our mouths work faster than our minds.

Yet another example occurred when I reviewed James Darren's summer concert in Marina Del Rey, California. James Darren first gained fame with his "Moondoggie" character in the *Gidget* films. He later starred in the TV series, *The Time Tunnel,* and in the film, *The Guns of Navarone,* among others. In addition to a successful acting career, he also directed films and recorded music. After the concert, Mr. Darren met with fans and signed autographs. I was there to ask a few questions. When he asked me my name, I said, "Francine." He smiled and said that was Gidget's real name in the films. Having grown up on the *Gidget* movies, I knew every line in the films, so I corrected him: "Actually it was Frances. She was also called Francie." I immediately blushed. Did I really correct Moondoggie? He smiled but didn't say anything. Thankfully, he let it go, but there were a few seconds when I wondered what he was going to say to me.

No matter how long you have been in this business, there will be a time when something comes out of your mouth that should have been left unsaid. How many times have you watched a live event unfolding on the news, and the anchors say dumb things to fill the air time? It's just part of what we do. When we journalists say something that might have been better left unsaid, the best thing to do is to ignore it, unless it needs clarification to get us out of a sticky situation. On the flipside, those being interviewed are in the same boat—you should hear some of the things they say!

Some celebrities reveal too much about their upcoming projects. During one phone conference with Donny and Marie Osmond before they started their new Las Vegas show, Marie was talking about some of their future projects and was about to spill the beans about something big. Donny, in his big-brother voice, cautioned, "Careful. Careful." It was clear that Marie felt very comfortable talking to us on the phone, and this was endearing to those of us on the other end of the line. Unfortunately, we never got to hear about the project she was going to reveal.

Some celebrities reveal too much about their personal lives. I was in one roundtable situation with Mandy Moore, an up-and-coming actress who was in a well-publicized relationship with Andy Roddick, a tennis star. She was gushing and grinning from ear to ear. Mandy explained to us that they were soulmates and were so happy together. There was no hiding her joy. Several months later, the couple went through a public break-up. When I saw that actress the next time, she commented that she would never again speak publicly about her personal life. She had learned her lesson.

Another actress, Hilary Swank, during the 2004 roundtable for the film, *Million Dollar Baby*, answered a question about her marriage to Chad Lowe and what kept them together. She said: "I would say communication and respect and believing in another person. I've been with my husband for over 12 years, and certainly that's what made our relationship work. We have a mutual respect; and like I said, the communication is I think key and believing in one another. That makes you feel like you can do anything." Unfortunately, this couple split in an awkward public display just a couple of years later.

In this chapter, journalists answer the question, "Have you ever asked a question or made a comment and immediately thought, *Why did I ask (say) that?*" My colleagues and I agree that no matter how accomplished you are at your job, there is always the chance that something will slip out of your mouth. It just happens. And you would be surprised at some of the things I have heard from both interviewers and interviewees over the years. Sometimes they are funny, and sometimes they are ridiculous. But slips of the tongue are part of being human. If we all had scripts from which to read, then think of how boring life would be!

Rob Owen, *Pittsburgh Post-Gazette*

Oh yeah. All the time. Sometimes it's a question that comes out wrong. Sometimes it's a question that's not thought through enough. Sometimes it's a question that I had prepared in advance that the person had just answered and I'm not editing my questions on the fly quickly enough. So yeah, there are plenty of times that I feel like an idiot after I've asked a question. You try to avoid those incidents, but we work so fast these days that sometimes they're going to slip through.

George Pennacchio, KABC-TV

Sometimes a question just doesn't come out right. If you're fast enough, you can say, "Wait—that's not what I meant to say!" and then re-phrase it in a way that actually makes sense! Have I unintentionally hurt feelings with a blunt question? I'm sure I have, but not on purpose. Sometimes, you can hit a nerve without knowing it.

Julio Martinez, *VIP Latino Magazine*, KPFK Radio

Yes. Two weeks ago, I interviewed Denise Crosby, who was in rehearsal for the play, *Revisiting Wildfire*. My mind went into remote mode, and I asked one of my stock questions: "Were you familiar with this play before being cast in it?" She replied: "That would have been impossible. This is a world premiere."

Sean Daly, *New York Post*

No. Unless of course you mean the time I asked Sean Penn what he thought about Madonna getting remarried. He nearly clocked me!

Stephen Whitty, *Star-Ledger*

Usually it's more "Why didn't I ask that?"—which is often due to time constraints.

Rick Bentley, *Fresno Bee*

Yes. And it always happens in a public forum. During a press conference to promote the new TV series, *Twins*, starring Sara Gilbert and Molly Stanton as sisters, I thought it would be interesting to ask them how they deal with their own siblings. The problem was the question started with, "Do you have any brothers or sisters?" The fact that Gilbert's sister Melissa has been acting for years made the question stupid.

Now, in press conferences I write out my questions. It's easier to deal with being stupid in one-to-one interviews.

Michael Lee, RadioFree.com

I've always believed that a question is only as good as the answer it receives. Sometimes you can have what you think is a brilliantly thought out and worded question, but if the interviewee decides to shrug and say, "Not really," then that question failed. By contrast, stumbling through a completely inane question sometimes leads to a highly entertaining answer, which often speaks to the interviewee's communication and PR skills. But in those instances of questions that lead nowhere, yes, I always wish I could take those back. Sometimes it's a simple matter of using a slightly different word to color your point. For example, I've learned through experience to use the word "antagonist" instead of "villain," only because some actors take a bit of offense to describing their characters as the latter.

Candace Havens, FYI Television

I've had times when the other person misunderstood what I was asking. A certain *That '70s Show* star, who wasn't Ashton Kutcher, yelled at me in the middle of a press conference. All I asked was if they stuck together when negotiating like the *Friends* stars did (the big jump in the pay grade had just happened on *Friends*). He thought I was asking them how much money they made, and he went off on me. People around me were laughing at him for being such a jerk.

Scott Pierce, *Salt Lake Tribune*

Yes, when I was trying to toss Adam Corolla a softball question about how he juggles all his jobs and got confused, thinking he had been in a sitcom that he wasn't in. When I attempted to mock myself for my own confusion, he took offense and started yelling and swearing at me. I completely didn't catch that he was actually angry—I genuinely thought it was a light-hearted exchange—until he went nuts.

Jacqueline Cutler, Tribune Media Services

I am sure I have. I have been doing this for 33 years, and I know that not every word that comes out of my mouth is gold.

Fred Topel, Crave Online

More often about a year later, if I'm going back to reference older material, I may think, "Why did I ask that?" It just shows you how much you grow and develop your craft that suddenly the angles you used to work seem irrelevant now.

Margie Barron, *Production Update*

I was fairly new to the press tour, and the ABC show *Peaks* was being promoted at a Century Plaza breakfast gat[her]... where the cast was mingling with the journalists. I wasn'[t] familiar with the stars of the show, but I saw this handsome y[oung] actor-type standing off to the side and started to talk to him a[bout] the show. Then I asked, "What role do you play?" He said, "I'm [the] head of the network." I think I told him that it's nice for an ac[tor] to dream big. But it was Bob Iger, and he remembered this a[nd] laughed when I retold it recently.

Hanh Nguyen, TVGuide.com

Take your pick: When I asked Toni Collette what she thought about her *In Her Shoes* character being the "plain" sister in the movie or asking a 20-year-old actress (who, to be fair, plays 15) if she was okay watching all the sex and nudity on one of her favorite shows.

Tim Riley, *Woodland Daily Democrat*

I am more likely to wonder why I didn't ask a particular question.

Winnie Bonelli, North Jersey Media Group

I asked Chuck Norris what was "the stupidest question anyone ever asked him?" He literally laughed, jumped up, grabbed me, and whirled me around, answering, "You just asked it."

Valerie Milano, *Hollywood Today*

Interviewing Lauren Zalzanick from Bravo—I can't remember exactly what I asked her, but her response was something like, "Why would you ask me that question?"

ansas City Star

Twin
ering
too
ung
out
he
or
d

empton was once profiled in *The New Yorker*
 s interviewing method, which he said consisted
 ιologues with a question tacked weakly onto the
 just "Don't you think?" And yet he was Murray
 was brilliant. So I give myself some grace for asking
 t ramble on or make me sound like a know-it-all.
 have learned from TCA press conferences that a
 tupid question can yield a revealing, thoughtful, or just
 nswer.

Walker, *New Orleans Times-Picayune*

Not really. Sometimes the weirdest questions result in a
le answer. I think interviewing is the most important part of
umn writing, and I usually overprepare.

Rob Salem, *Toronto Star*

Yes, and the reason is always, "desperation." The worst one
that I always hate myself for, but it is sometimes a necessary evil, is
the old "What drew you to this project?" In second place, "Where
do you see yourself in 10 years?"

Alex Strachan, *Postmedia News*

Not really. Perhaps when I'm very tired, or the interview subject isn't that interesting and my mind is on cruise control. I've
never regretted asking a dumb question in that situation, though.
It's more a case of, "Forget it, this is pointless, you're boring—not
even Kurt Vonnegut could get anything out of this, so let's move
on."

9

How Rude!

People are not always considerate. Let's face it, we have all come across someone who has done or said something that rubs us the wrong way. Journalists and celebrities can both come across as rude and insensitive. In business situations, these times are definitely uncalled for.

Sometimes celebrities put journalists in uncomfortable situations. I once attended a press junket at a Pasadena hotel, which is now called The Langham. I had completed all of the roundtables except the last one. When the final actress entered, she sat down at the head of the table and inquired if anyone minded if she smoked. I said I did, as I am very allergic to cigarette smoke. She said, "Well, I'm French," and began to light up her cigarette. I was shocked and replied, "Well, I'm out of here." I retrieved my recorder and briefcase and walked out. She wasn't worth getting a migraine. Later, when I told the publicist what had happened and why I would not be including that actress in any articles about the film, the publicist said I had done the right thing. After all, this woman could have waited the fifteen or twenty minutes it took to finish the session.

I later encountered the same situation, but with a different result. I was waiting to interview Jonathan Rhys Meyers in a hotel room. He walked in and asked if he could smoke. I informed him that it would definitely bother me, and I would not be able to stay in the room if he did. He smiled and said he thought he could make it twenty minutes without a cigarette. I chuckled and told him that if he couldn't, then he was in a lot of trouble. He was fine through the interview, and I appreciated his courtesy. We both left happy with a successful interview under our belts.

Sometimes celebrities are inconsiderate. One time, I was supposed to conduct a phone interview with an actor in New York. We scheduled the time via his publicist. My mother was in the hospital at the time, so I had to make sure I was in the hospital lobby at the appointed time—cell phones were not allowed in patients' rooms. I waited and waited for the call, but it didn't come. I called the publicist. She told me that she would get back to me in a few minutes. When she did, she said that the actor had forgotten about the interview and wanted to reschedule. We did, and the same thing happened! The publicist wanted to reschedule a third time, but I declined. I wasn't going to leave my mom's side for an actor who might or might not remember to call me.

Sometimes celebrities are just plain grumpy. I once asked Harrison Ford how Hollywood had changed from the time he started acting in films. I expected to hear something about the technology of special effects. Instead, he looked me right in the eyes and said with a stern, condescending tone, "I don't live in Hollywood." Another journalist jumped in quickly to clarify the question was about the business of Hollywood, not the actual location. I thought perhaps he was just having a bad day, but after Ford left the room, several of my colleagues informed me that he was notorious for being sharp with the press and had a reputation of not being forthcoming during interviews. That's something I learned the hard way.

Sometimes, though, celebrities with reputations for being difficult can pleasantly surprise you. If I know in advance that someone has a penchant for being rude during interviews, I will try to find some common ground. For example, Ryan O'Neal is notorious for having a short temper during interviews. I was interviewing him for the film, *Malibu's Most Wanted,* and I knew that, like me, he had recently suffered from cancer. I asked him about his cancer the first chance I got, framing the question with my experience from a few years earlier. From then on, he was very nice and, I dare say, charming. I thoroughly enjoyed our entire interview.

The same experience occurred with Ashley Judd in a roundtable. I had been told she was not always happy to talk to the press. I tried to find something she was interested in, so I asked her about her sister and whether Wynonna had been approached to record a song for the 2004 film, *De-Lovely.* I followed up with a couple more questions about Wynonna and also Ashley's singing. She lit up like a candle. We had a very nice interview, and she even came over to say hello and ask how I was doing the next day when I was at the hotel for another press junket. Ashley Judd turned out to be one of my favorite interviewees.

Interviewees are not the only ones who can be curt or rude. Journalists can be overbearing. During one roundtable for *De-Lovely,* I really wanted to ask Kevin Kline a question. But every time I started to pose my question, another journalist—who was bigger and much louder—took over the conversation. He commandeered much of the roundtable, and my frustration grew by the minute. Finally, another journalist scolded him and told him to let me ask my question. I was both embarrassed and excited as Kevin Kline looked over to me and held up his hand, gesturing that no one else should speak while I asked my question. As a matter of fact, several times during the duration of the roundtable, Mr. Kline looked directly at me. Everyone knew that I then had the floor!

Journalists can also be prying. As the public becomes more enamored with the personal lives of celebrities, there are more and more tabloid-style questions. Those of us who are at junkets to get information about the films are not there to find out what designer a particular actress likes the best or who makes her favorite shoes—but many journalists are. This is even more prevalent when younger actors are involved. During the press conference for the 2005 film, *Herbie Fully Loaded,* many journalists in attendance directed a lot of personal questions to Lindsay Lohan, who had recently been in the hospital. My friends and I felt badly for Lindsay and steered the questions back to the subject of the movie. After the press conference, the studio publicist came over to me and thanked me for trying to keep the questions on the subject at hand.

For this chapter, journalists were asked, "Has anyone ever been rude to you while you were on the job?" The stories my colleagues have to tell about this aspect of our business are pretty interesting. Read on.

Dave Walker, *New Orleans Times-Picayune*

Jerry Lewis kind of snapped at me during a TV Press Tour interview session when I asked a follow-up question about his role in the *2011 MDA Telethon.* I thought my questions were respectful. It was a TV event. I write about TV. The Telethon airs on TV. It was a natural series of questions. His responses and attitude were widely reported, and a few days later MDA announced that his already limited role had been completely eliminated. I doubt anything he said resulted in the action, but I'm still kind of sad about it. His work on the Telethon had been erratic, but his work on behalf of MDA has been heroic.

Stephen Whitty, *Star-Ledger*

Morgan Freeman and Tommy Lee Jones were rude. Lauren Bacall was pleasant to me but rude to everyone else around her; so was Christopher Guest. Spike Lee can be rude. Jennifer Lopez was in full diva mode at the time I met her. That's fine. It's all part of the story. Interviews with friendly people are good, and interviews with unfriendly people are good—it's the interviews with incredibly dull, completely rehearsed people that are a pain!

George Pennacchio, KABC-TV

Yes, but not often. Here's one example: I was interviewing a famous daytime TV "couple," and the interview just went south. By the time it was over, we all just walked away without saying a word, and they cancelled 25 interviews set for the next day. Since then, though, those fences have been mended, and I've enjoyed talking with both of them on other occasions, and it's all been very nice.

Margie Barron, *Production Update*

Mostly the personal publicists handling the stars are the ones who are rude. A recent example is that I had asked an actor a question and he was giving me a lengthy intelligent answer. His publicist was hovering and started to poke at me, telling me to "wrap it up." After poking me once too often, I turned to her and said, "Do you want me to tell him to shut up, he's talking too much?" The actor looked horrified at the publicist's conduct.

Hanh Nguyen, TVGuide.com

Horrifying. For my first red carpet ever I went to the *Cheaper by the Dozen* remake premiere and asked Bonnie Hunt if the movie made her want to plan on having kids. I don't tend to ask those questions normally, but I was green, and it just sort of came out. I figured, "Eh, it's a throwaway question. She can just say, 'Someday, you never know,' and we can move on." Well, apparently, she was offended, and said, "Well, that's quite personal! Did you have sex last night?" trying to turn the tables on me. I was working freelance for MaryKateandAshley.com at the time. It's not quite the response I expected from a seasoned actress talking to a young reporter working for a tween site.

Jacqueline Cutler, Tribune Media Services

Yes. A famous actor behaved so boorishly that the interview was useless. And P. Diddy's people were so disorganized that they canceled and rescheduled six times. The night before, I read a publicist the riot act. I had already interviewed Phylicia Rashad and Audra McDonald for the story. Both were on time, and I had enough to write the piece. The publicist swore to me that the interview was the next day at 1:30. I called at 1:29 and was put on hold. I vowed to myself that he had half an hour, and if he did not get on the phone that was it. He got on after 29 minutes. The interview was okay. But at the end, I told him that he did not become as wealthy as he is by breaking appointments six times and making people wait for half an hour. I told him that this was rude and unacceptable. He apologized profusely and promised to never do this to a journalist again. To be fair, I am not sure that he knew at all about the many changes. The next day, I received the loveliest bouquet and a handwritten apology letter.

Alex Strachan, *Postmedia News*

Not really. Usually, on those rare occasions it does happen, it's someone very low on the totem pole. The third lead in a new drama that's destined to go two episodes and out, or a not-very-important sportscaster with a swelled head and misplaced sense of their own self-importance. At TCA parties, it's usually a case of the person saying, "Can I get something to eat first?" and then you never see them again. What amazes me (and this is a constant) is that it's always the lesser lights who pull off that routine, never the Hugh Lauries of the world.

Brian Sebastian, Movie Reviews & More

Former Black Panther Bobby Seale. He is still angry from the '60s. He was promoting *The Chicago 10* for PBS, and I was the only

Black person interviewing him. He was in a bad mood. I had to wait 45 minutes for him. He didn't want to miss his flight back to San Francisco, and I guess no one told him he had an interview to do, so he came down in a mood and he just didn't want to answer any questions. He left a bad taste in my mouth. I was doing him a favor, and he took it out on me like I was taking his money away!

Winnie Bonelli, North Jersey Media Group

Slash from Guns 'n Roses, who was totally bored and really didn't want to do the interview. He kept yawning.

Sean Daly, *New York Post*

Harrison Ford is the rudest a-hole in show business. Followed possibly by Tommy Lee Jones. I have actually seen Ford call reporters out for asking what he thinks are "stupid questions." Sometimes it is fun when the subject is a dick.

Back in 1985, I was doing a telephone interview with Peter Tork of The Monkees. At the time the band was on its 20th anniversary tour. I asked at the end of the call if I could come backstage and meet him in person when the band got to Syracuse. He said "No!" Then he explained that if I came backstage I would ask him for an autograph (which I assured him I wouldn't). He insisted I would. He told me that I would never be able to live it down if I didn't—that I had to have a sister or mother or girlfriend who would insist on getting his autograph because The Monkees were the most popular band in the history of music—next to only The Beatles. Needless to say, I did not go backstage and never met him, but I wrote a lengthy article about what a jerk he is.

Ten years later I happened to be in Rochester, NY with my then-girlfriend to see a touring stage show called *The Real Live Brady Bunch*. They recreated episodes of *The Brady Bunch* on stage. And that night it was the episode where Davy Jones went with Marsha to the prom. The real Davy Jones was a special guest star. After the show, we were in the hotel bar, and Davy Jones walked in. So I sent him and his friend a round of shots. A few minutes later, they called last call. Davy Jones walked over to me, said thank you for the drinks, and asked if I knew another bar in the area. So we all went together. We ended up drinking until four in the morning. But I will never forget skipping down the streets of Rochester, drunk, at four in the morning, arm in arm with Davy Jones singing, "Hey, hey, we're The Monkees."

Julio Martinez, *VIP Latino Magazine*, KPFK Radio

Mickey Rooney was relentlessly rude and condescending while nude, when I interviewed him in 1988 during his tour of *A Funny Thing Happened on the Way to the Forum.*

Bonnie Siegler, Freelance

One of my editors wanted me to ask Jane Fonda about her plastic surgery when Fonda wasn't even admitting to having any done. While I told my editor I didn't think it such a good question, she wanted it done, anyway. So I waited till the end of the interview and weaved it into the conversation. Jane pushed her chair away from the desk and basically said, "It's none of anybody's f-ing business whether I had plastic surgery done or not. And this interview is over." And it was!

Howard Benjamin, Interview Factory Radio Networks

There have been too many to count, but when you consider that I've conducted more than 50,000 interviews, the percentages are very low. Having said that, a few years ago I spoke with the band Train and during the course of the interview I brought up the fact that the first time I ever heard one of the band's songs was on an episode of *Party of Five* and it was their song, "Free." At that point the band's lead singer, Patrick Monahan, looked at me and said, "You've never seen an episode of *Party of Five* in your life, don't BS me." I took that moment to inform him that as a member of the Television Critics Association since 1986, I have watched more television than most of the people he knows combined. He quickly realized that I knew what I was talking about and never again questioned anything I said.

Meg Mimura, *Lighthouse*

If being drunk and not being able to remember what I just asked counts, yes. It was excruciatingly painful to sit face to face and try to get some kind of coherent answers from this drunk lady. And this happened at the second one-on-one electronic junket I ever attended. It felt like an hour, and was I glad to get out of the room!

Donald Sutherland was rude and mean to a young guy from Australia. "What am I supposed to do with this?" said grouchy Sutherland and tossed a stuffed animal the guy brought all the way from Down Under. The guy came out of the room crying and told me what had happened. I went in after this tiff, and as soon as I sat down I asked Sutherland what money meant to him (this is when he was in *Dirty Sexy Money*). After a long pause, he gave an uneasy, run-of-the mill answer. Sutherland wasn't ready for a philosophical question and was apparently in a terrible fluster. Got you! What you put out comes back all the time, no matter what. Although a few years later, I found out the young guy was not a professional reporter but someone who won a sweepstakes to act as a video journalist. He sure had a Hollywood experience, didn't he?

Rick Bentley, *Fresno Bee*

If they have, I don't remember it. You have to remember that I get to talk to celebrities when they have something to promote. That means they are going to be on their best behavior. What's been surprising is how cordial celebrities with bad reputations have been.

I was working at the *Bakersfield Californian* when I got word that Sean Penn had checked in at a local motel. He was in town to look at some property he was thinking about buying. A call was made to the motel and a message left. The idea was that I could at least tell my editor I had tried to reach him for an interview. Imagine my surprise a few hours later when Penn called. He was very polite in turning down the interview. The fact he even called me back says that at least part of his bad-boy image isn't deserved.

Rob Owen, *Pittsburgh Post-Gazette*

Yes, or an attempted interview. We tried to interview an actress at a UPN party. We were actually going up to interview her sort of as a pity interview because nobody was talking to her. And we felt like that was unfortunate. You do feel sorry for these folks when they show up to these parties at press tour and nobody wants to talk to the stars because the show is deemed not worthy or something. It was Linda Park on *Star Trek Enterprise*. So we went up to her to do essentially a pity interview and she was like, "No. I'm not doing interviews." And that always annoys me. You are an actor at a press party. You are there to do interviews. And I remember Gillian Anderson did the same thing early on in *The X-Files*. She showed up at a party and said, "No. I'm here to spend time with Chris Carter." Part of their job is doing press, and I think sometimes actors don't recognize that's part of their job. Those were attempts at interviews that never happened because the actors were pulling an attitude.

Michael Lee, RadioFree.com

I don't think I've ever had someone be rude to me directly, especially since actors are conditioned to be on their best behavior around the media. But like anyone, I'm sure I've had bad days where my interview questions suck, and the talent has simply tolerated me. I have, though, seen talent be rude to fans and waiters, and

I've seen talent be rude in the sense that they will put down other people's point of views or beliefs as a way to soapbox their own personal agendas.

Fred Topel, Crave Online

Once or twice, and I wouldn't give those people the publicity of mentioning them. Usually the talent are on good behavior, so my overwhelming impression is that filmmakers are nice!

Candace Havens, FYI Television

Anthony Geary was on a panel, and afterward no one was talking to him. I went over to say "hi," and then I realized why no one had bothered to talk to him.

Tim Riley, *Woodland Daily Democrat*

Even in a casual setting, I found Will Ferrell and John Goodman not to be very pleasant to talk to during a TCA Press Tour. It was the feeling you get when someone is looking over your shoulder to spot a better opportunity.

Scott Pierce, *Salt Lake Tribune*

Yeah. There was that whole Adam Corolla thing. (See Chapter 8.) Again, he was profane and out of control and, hand to God, I was trying to toss him a softball question.

Gerri Miller, Freelance

I can't recall specifics other than the time I interviewed Swedish guitarist Yngwie Malmsteen years ago, and he gave one-word answers to everything. And the roundtable with John Goodman when he basically did the same, making it obvious he'd rather have been anywhere but in a room with journalists.

10

Off the Record

Sometimes it's precisely when the cameras and tape recorders are off that you wish you had recorded a moment—something said, something done, or something experienced. But sometimes my colleagues and I relish the off-camera moments so we can "get real."

All entertainment journalists have experiences they wish they had recorded. One of mine involves Robin Williams. I clearly remember one morning when ten of us were sitting at a roundtable waiting for Robin Williams to come in. We knew he was near the room, because we could hear him in the hallway. As he entered the room, he said in his best comedic voice, "Oh, good. A *minyan*." For those who do not know, a *minyan* is a group of ten adults required for a religious service in Judaism. It may sound only mildly clever now, but with Robin Williams's delivery, it was absolutely hysterical.

The time I most regret not having my tape recorder turned on was just before an interview with Shirley MacLaine. It was for her book *Sage-ing while Age-ing*, which was published in 2008. My husband had driven me, and we were early, as usual. The publicist had us wait in an adjoining room where there were drinks and snacks. A few minutes later, Shirley MacLaine walked in and came immediately into the room, where we were sitting at a small table. She sat down, and we began talking. I mentioned that I had experienced many unexplainable situations or occurrences and was anxious to talk to her about them. She and I immediately started discussing paranormal experiences. Well, my husband, being a man who does not go in for all that "hooey," rolled his eyes while Ms. MacLaine and I were conversing. She saw his expression, and I was completely embarrassed. But it didn't affect Shirley at all. She said he was just not in tune with things as I was. Since then, I have interviewed Ms. MacLaine on numerous occasions and always have my tape recorder on. She always has something fascinating to say.

Off-camera moments can happen due to technological difficulties. After I completed a one-on-one interview with a director and was heading back to my car, I decided to check my recording and discovered that I had accidentally set my tape recorder to "play" instead of "record." I hurried home and ran into the house yelling, "Don't talk to me. I have to get to my computer *fast*." I immediately began typing everything I could remember, word for word. Then for what I didn't recall on a word-for-word basis, I took out my notes and my list of questions and typed out everything that I remembered. It was panic time, but it turned out all right in the end. After the article was published in the newspaper, I received an email from the director telling me how much he enjoyed my article.

Off-camera moments can occur at a celebrity's request. At a TCA cocktail party, I was talking to an actress. We were having an informal conversation and discussing our summer plans. She mentioned they were going to Mexico, and she was not a good traveler. She gets nervous on airplanes. I do too, so I told her to get some Xanax. To my surprise, she said she takes it when she flies. But then she said quickly, "Don't print that." Her family had been in the press numerous times for drug and alcohol addiction, and they didn't need any ammunition to fuel the fire. I assured her I wouldn't print the comment. After all, we white-knuckled fliers need to stick together!

Off-camera moments can also happen when we don't identify a journalistic gem. During one TCA Press Tour evening event, I was waiting for America Ferrera, the star of *Ugly Betty*, to finish with another interviewer before approaching her for some comments. While I waited, I started a conversation with a young man who I thought was also waiting for an interview with the actress. He later introduced himself as America's boyfriend. What an interesting article I could have written, had I only known to whom I was talking!

While entertainment journalists rue when celebrities' funny moments aren't captured on camera, they relish the time behind the scenes to say what they won't dare write. One day, we had a press junket with a veteran actor, who was part of the ensemble cast. I won't tell you who it was, but his father was also a famous actor. He was a delight to interview—a very nice guy who provided us with a lot of information. But when he left, the conversation in our room went something like this:

"Did you see his forehead?"

"Yeah. Nothing moved."

"He must have just come from Botox."

"He must have a gallon of Botox in his face."

Often you'll hear, "He looks good for his age." "You can tell she had a lot of plastic surgery." "Was he drunk?" "I would love to own that dress." "He looks much older in person than on-screen." "What a jerk." "His eyes are so blue." "That was a great session." "He shouldn't have come if he wasn't going to say anything." "This movie is so bad, they shouldn't even have any interviews." Of course, we would never write something like that—or we wouldn't be invited back to the roundtables!

As many of my friends and colleagues relate in this chapter, off-camera moments are often very comical—and they are what make us popular at parties! For this chapter, journalists were asked, "What funny or interesting things have happened when the recorders or cameras were not on?"

Candace Havens, FYI Television

I was once talking to a younger star at a party. He stumbled a bit and knocked some of the desserts off the table. We sort of pushed everything under the tablecloth. Then we ran to a corner of the room far away.

Gerri Miller, Freelance

Well, not so funny, but realizing that the interview didn't record. It's happened more times than I'd care to admit.

George Pennacchio, KABC-TV

I was once mooned by a star of daytime television.

Bonnie Siegler, Freelance

I was waiting to interview Ed O'Neill on the set of *Married . . . with Children* and had my parents with me visiting from NY. After the cameras stopped rolling and I had my time with O'Neill (who played a shoe salesman on the show), my dad went up to him and said, "I'm a shoe man, too." Ed O'Neill politely asked where, as if he really were a shoe salesman. I was totally embarrassed.

Howard Benjamin, Interview Factory Radio Networks

There was a notorious heavy metal band that I accompanied my wife to interview. The band was late—what's new?—and we were asked to wait in the hotel bar while they got things together. After almost an hour and a half, we were escorted to their room, and we could see that their mind was on "when will the drugs get here" and not on the interview. Undaunted, the interview began, and my wife's first question was, "In a business that forgets you in ten minutes, what do you attribute your fifteen years of longevity to?" Without a beat came the answer, "Cocaine." I should mention that also in the room was a former band member that even though he had been reminded several times that we were recording for broadcast, kept yelling obscenities at every opportunity. My wife had had enough and told them to focus on the interview or she would pack up her recorder and leave. Again without a beat came the response, "Good—that means we can get loaded as soon as the drugs get here." We left! It's funny now, but at the time it was a total waste of time.

Several years later, I spoke to that same former band member and told him what had gone down the first time. He turned out to be one of the most cooperative people I have ever met and swore that he'd never have a repeat performance like that again.

Julio Martinez, *VIP Latino Magazine*, KPFK Radio

I interviewed Charo in her dressing room. She invited me to sit down while she finished talking to her hair stylist. I accidentally sat on one of her support bras, and it bruised my butt.

David Sheehan, Hollywood Close-Ups, Inc.

John Travolta took off his shirt and gave it to me—because he was borrowing one of my shirts, since he didn't like the way he looked in his own T-shirt and wanted to make a better presentation. This was back in the '70s, just before he was Oscar nominated for *Saturday Night Fever*. In those days, you could get the stars to come to your studio, long before the "junkets," where everyone gathers in one hotel.

Hanh Nguyen, TVGuide.com

Lindsay Lohan did pushups after her *Just My Luck* press conference to prove how strong she was. She really didn't do that many.

Margie Barron, *Production Update*

Anjelica Huston was at the Gene Autry Western Museum, where there was a party for *Lonesome Dove*. She walked into the reception looking like she was unapproachable. No one would go up to her, because they thought she was difficult or uncooperative. But I wanted to get a few quotes, so I was the only one to walk up to her and start chatting—and Anjelica's face broke into the biggest smile. She was so sweet and happy to answer questions. We laughed about a lot of things before we did a little interview. So I found out that her icy image is not really the person she is.

Rob Owen, *Pittsburgh Post-Gazette*

This wasn't funny, but it was memorable. When interviewing Carrie Brownstein of *Portlandia*, my recorder malfunctioned and I didn't get any of the interview on tape. I had to ask to chat with her a second time. That was mortifying. I'd never had a recorder malfunction in 15 years of doing interviews.

Valerie Milano, *Hollywood Today*

During the interview with the creators of *I Hate My Teenage Daughter*, the ladies started asking me questions, since they only had boys and I have a fourteen-year-old daughter. They asked me "What's a great line that she has said?" I told them she made her dad a Father's Day card that said, "I know we don't get along all the time, but don't forget, I am a teenager." The creators told me that was the best line of the evening and wanted to use it for the show.

Rob Salem, *Toronto Star*

I'm told I spilled a cocktail all over Matt Groening, though I don't remember ever doing that. Which I guess speaks to the likelihood of it actually having happened.

I'll tell you the short version of how I met Lucy Lawless, who really has become a good friend. Like every man alive and many homosexual women, I've had a crush on her since her *Xena* days. When she was in Toronto shooting the short-lived *Tarzan* series, I recruited her to sing at the annual Gilda's Club charity gala, which she did (and, denied time for rehearsal, blew the lyrics to a Bare Naked Ladies tune). I was mortified for her, but she shrugged it off like a champ and totally charmed a theatre full of patrons who had paid a fortune for tickets.

Afterwards the performers all agreed to cast their handprints in plaster to sell for extra funds. Lucy offered to do her boobs. I got to stand guard outside the washroom. Some guy from out of town bought 'em for $5,000. Any wonder I love this woman?

Oh wait, I just thought of another one. I'm 19 years old and sent to interview Pat Boone. Like I give a crap. I tape the thing, not even listening to what he's saying. Get back to the office. Nothing recorded. Nothing remembered. Totally screwed. So I made it up— hey, I was 19. We all do stupid stuff at that age. Two weeks later, I get a letter, and I know it is from Boone because the word "Pat" is embossed on it in two-inch, high-raised gold letters. Rather formal for a summons, I thought. But this is what it said—I swear to God, verbatim: "Just wanted to thank you for one of the most enjoyable and accurate interviews I've ever had."

Brian Sebastian, Movie Reviews & More

I was doing a TV interview with Angie Harmon, and she had a black cast on her hand. Without me saying anything, she says, "I hurt my hand masturbating." Without missing a beat, I say to her, "I have a lot of female friends who would love to show you how!" She sat there in silence.

Michael Lee, RadioFree.com

I visited a movie set where lunch was being served in a stuffy, poorly ventilated basement, and one of the actors described the smell as "a hot hurricane of ass crack," if I remember correctly. I don't know, but I got a huge kick out of the sudden, impromptu comment. And now I think that actor should write a blog or column, or at least take a side job writing for raunchy fortune cookies.

Scott Pierce, *Salt Lake Tribune*

Back in the early 1990s, I had occasion to interview Valerie Bertinelli several times. I am six days older than her; her son is 14 days older than my boy-girl twins. We were at a TCA party exchanging baby pictures in 1992, when she says, "Edward! Edward! Look at these babies! They're the same age as Wolfie." So Eddie Van Halen takes my wallet and looks at pictures of all three of my kids.

My kids love that story.

Alex Strachan, *Postmedia News*

In terms of funny things happening during interviews, it's usually just the to-and-fro of conversation, especially when you're talking with someone who's naturally witty, like Hugh Laurie. It's probably his Oxbridge background, but Laurie has a way of making every second thought sound funny. And human nature. This past January, for example, I had a laugh when, outside on the veranda at the Pasadena Langham during a one-on-one with Jeremy Irons, he stood up and looked over the ledge to drop the ash of his cigarette. He saw the ledge directly overlooked the restaurant and stopped in the nick of time. That was funny as hell—but, as I say, it was a spontaneous, unplanned moment that was pure human behavior. I really enjoyed talking with Jeremy Irons. I suppose, as with Laurie, it's an English theatre thing. They're very witty, erudite, and well-spoken with very quick, lively minds. One hardly has to work at an interview; you just have to come up with semi-interesting questions, and off they go.

Sean Daly, *New York Post*

Too long a story to tell you here, but I inadvertently ended up in an episode of *Nick & Jessica: Newlyweds* after stopping by their house for an interview.

Jacqueline Cutler, Tribune Media Services

Snooki recently did my hair and made a pouf. She made me promise that I would keep it in. I went to synagogue that evening still wearing it.

Winnie Bonelli, North Jersey Media Group

I guess being propositioned by Steven Tyler of Aerosmith after he dropped his jeans to show me a bruise he got from a fall. I teased him about it years later when I interviewed him again. He sort of gasped and asked if we had sex. I replied, "No, but you were a perfect gentleman and very sweet about it."

Another time I interviewed singer Paul Anka, who invited me and a girlfriend, Maureen, to his concert the following evening at a New Jersey amphitheater. The three of us hung out backstage until his helicopter showed up to whisk him away to Manhattan. Meanwhile, we had to get the car that was parked out front. Everything was pitch black, and an eight-foot fence stood between us and the car. We both wore skirts. Maureen started to jump when she exclaimed, "Don't peek," I replied. "You've got to be kidding. 'Don't peek?' I'm more worried about breaking my neck."

Dave Walker, *New Orleans Times-Picayune*

I got to spend some time with Billy Crystal and Louie Anderson in New Orleans when they were filming stuff for a Comic Relief special aiding Hurricane Katrina recovery. Watching both interact with folks in flood-ravaged parts of the city was pretty cool. Crystal played catch football with some kids on the street and interviewed people who were trying to rebuild. It was a great couple of days. Another: I was spending time on a location shoot for *True Blood* in Clinton, LA—standing in for Bon Temps—and a baby bat fell out of a tree. The crew medic called a specialist, and they were able to nurse it back to health. After a few hours, it flew away.

11

Interview Funnies

Celebrities can be sidesplitting. Many of them have quick wits, engaging personalities, and amazing stories to tell. A joke will put everyone at ease, and an interesting story will captivate a crowd. Like most of us, I enjoy being entertained during interviews—and celebrities are experts at entertaining.

Celebrities are often naturally funny people, and no one is funnier than Robin Williams. During a roundtable with Robin, a colleague had forgotten to turn off her cell phone. To her horror, it rang right in the middle of the roundtable. Thoroughly embarrassed, she fumbled frantically for the phone to turn it off. Robin told her to answer the phone call, which was from her mother. Suddenly, Robin snatched the phone and began to talk with her mother, Robin Williams-style. What a thrill for my friend's mother! And what a relief for my friend. Robin's quick wit and funny personality took the heat off of her mistake.

In addition to natural wit, celebrities entertain a crowd with vivid and captivating stories. Some of the juiciest are the ones that divulge a little too much about another celebrity. My interview with James Garner is a perfect example. A few of us were gathered at a roundtable interviewing James about his role in the 2004 film, *The Notebook*. James discussed the film then opened up about his legendary career. He told us how Steve McQueen gave filmmakers a headache on the set of the 1963 movie, *The Great Escape*. Steve didn't like his part, so he threatened to leave. James took Steve over to his house in Munich, Germany, to have a heart-to-heart that went something like this:

"What's your problem, Steve?"

"Well, I don't like a lot of the scenes."

"This is silly. You don't like anything, Steve. You want to be the hero, but you don't want to do anything heroic."

Apparently, Steve McQueen didn't want to do anything physically challenging in the movie. So the filmmakers rewrote the script.

It's not often that you hear about the drama that goes on behind the cameras, and we at the roundtable were enthralled. James enjoyed his captive audience so much that he told a publicist to back off when it was time to finish the roundtable. He also dished about his female costars. He enjoyed working with Sally Field, Doris Day, Audrey Hepburn, Shirley MacLaine, and Julie Andrews. But he thought another very famous female co-star was a diva who cared more about how she looked than what was in the script. We were shocked, awed, and begged for more!

Celebrities don't have to dish the dirt to keep us interested—there is plenty of entertainment value in any type of personal story. Julie Andrews once told me about a *Sound of Music* get-together, where everyone came dressed as a character from the film. She looked around the room and saw a man dressed entirely in yellow. Julie approached him and asked, "Who are you supposed to be?"

"I'm Ray, a drop of golden sun," was the reply.

In this chapter, journalists were asked, "What is the funniest thing that has happened during an interview?" As you're about to read, interview funnies happen all the time.

David Sheehan, Hollywood Close-Ups, Inc.

Marlon Brando throwing the cardboard coffee cup at me, not realizing there was still some coffee in it.

Howard Benjamin, Interview Factory Radio Networks

At the end of every interview, we do these quick station liners, like, "I'm so-and-so, and you're listening to the greatest station in the nation, so stay right here!" Most of the time the talent launch right into reading them with little or no reservation, but in the case of George Clooney, he had a moment of confusion and read the line wrong. That led to laughter throughout the room, and after what seemed to be several minutes, he was able to compose himself long enough to finish the liners.

Also there was another time I showed up at a singer's home, and she greeted me at the door wearing only a towel. I told her I thought it was best that she get dressed before we begin. She looked at me like I was crazy, and come to think of it, I probably was.

Rick Bentley, *Fresno Bee*

Interviews at the Television Critics Association meetings generally start with a press conference. Afterward, reporters and talent end up in an interview scrum to get material to make your story different.

The scrum for the launch of the ABC series *Ugly Betty* was particularly tight. I noticed while I was interviewing Salma Hayek that she was being pushed closer and closer to me. While this wasn't a bad thing, the best course seemed to be to back up to give her room. I immediately noticed I was cheek-to-cheek with someone. All I could do was figure the journalist behind me was going to ignore the close proximity also. When I finished talking with Hayek, I turned to leave. That's when I noticed I was standing back-to-back with Vanessa Williams. Being squeezed between such talented and attractive women is a memorable moment.

Donna Plesh, Thecolumnists.com

Halfway through an interview, I discovered my recorder was not working. I was looking at the talent responding to my questions and did not see that the red "on" button on the recorder was not lit. So I wound up with only half of an interview, because I was certainly not going to ask the talent the same questions over again.

Rob Owen, *Pittsburgh Post-Gazette*

When *Dharma & Greg* premiered, I was working for the *Albany Times Union*. Actress Susan Sullivan grew up near Albany, so I had to interview her for the paper. After the interview, she asked me, in a conspiratorial voice, "What do you think our chances are, and what about the other shows?" I liked the *Dharma* pilot and said I thought the show would do well. It did, and forever after whenever I see her—most recently on the set of *Castle*—she always remembers me and says I was her good luck charm for *Dharma*. That's obviously not true—the show stood on its own two feet quite well—but it is funny to be remembered that way when so often actors look at members of the press as disposable. To be remembered is refreshing.

Fred Topel, Crave Online

At a roundtable with Hilary Swank, a journalist had a coughing fit so bad that he started choking. Hilary stopped talking to make sure he was okay. He was, he got a drink and settled, but he must have been embarrassed to have had to stop the interview.

Valerie Milano, *Hollywood Today*

Writing for *Genesis* magazine and being alone in a hotel room with the nude Ted Nugent for an interview after his concert. Well, he was in bed with a woman, and I was a little uncomfortable, to say the least. But a whole lot of fun.

Michael Lee, RadioFree.com

It doesn't happen often, but I'm always amused when a fight breaks out. I guess long afternoons of sitting in hospitality suites at five-star hotels eating free food can make even the most even-keeled amongst us snap, and that manic energy has to spill over somehow. Reporters generally won't come to blows or cut someone, but they'll throw a hissy fit and maybe even write about it later on. How is that not comedy?

Candace Havens, FYI Television

Ricky Gervais has a habit of making Diet Coke go through my nose. Oh, and Shirley MacLaine's dog insisted I pet it while we talked.

George Pennacchio, KABC-TV

I was interviewing Gary Oldman once when we both got uncontrollable giggles over something silly we'd talked about before the interview began. Almost my entire piece, when aired, was two men unable to speak because we couldn't stop laughing. It was actually fun to watch—even if it told you almost nothing about the movie he was promoting.

Also, I was interviewing Andie MacDowell for *Groundhog Day* years ago, and I was asking about her slapping Bill Murray in a scene—and how many times did she have to do it, and did it ever hurt.

She said, "Would you like me to slap you?"
Stupidly, I said, "Sure."
And she did.
And it hurt.
And I laughed.

Scott Pierce, *Salt Lake Tribune*

I don't know that it's the funniest, but I was once interviewing Jimmy Smits and, during the course of the conversation, I told him how my teenage son was a huge fan of him on *The West Wing*. I told him how we had kept the sixth-season finale on the DVR all summer long and watched it at least once a week until the show returned that fall. I was sort of shocked when Jimmy gave me a hug.

Gerri Miller, Freelance

Robin Williams spent an entire roundtable doing hilarious shtick—voices, jokes, the whole nine, keeping us all in stitches— but there wasn't a single usable quote from the whole thing!

Julio Martinez, *VIP Latino Magazine*, KPFK Radio

I interviewed impressionist Rich Little prior to a rehearsal for a TV special. He was completely made up to look like Ronald Reagan. I think I asked him what comes first, the voice or the physical mannerisms. He said the physical characteristics. He gestured with his hand to show me a typical Reagan mannerism, and his wig fell off right onto his outstretched finger.

Winnie Bonelli, North Jersey Media Group

I was interviewing Kurt Russell, and he was relating how he loves to catch actors off-guard those few seconds after they flub a line. Then looking unflinchingly in my eyes he said, "That's what I love about bringing a woman to orgasm, when she loses total control." I knew he was doing it on purpose, so I kept right on writing, but I wore a hole in the notebook.

Brian Sebastian, Movie Reviews & More

I was scheduled to do an interview for *A Love Song for Bobby Long* at 12:05. I thought it was a strange time to do a radio interview. It turns out it was a five-minute TV slot and no one told me. I'm wearing sweats and a sweater, and it's a two-camera shoot. So without missing a beat, I turn into "TV Brian" with no makeup and (even though I don't like the film) I get one of my best TV interviews ever: John Travolta. After I finish my interview, he says that was one of *his* best interviews ever!

Jacqueline Cutler, Tribune Media Services

George Clooney played a prank on me. This was a few years back, and Clooney was still on *ER*. He was directing a live version of *Fail Safe*. I had interviewed Rod Steiger for a different story. What should have been a 20-minute interview turned into about 90 minutes. Mr. Steiger was hard of hearing and had a terrible phone. I have a soft voice, and he kept telling me to talk louder. I did until I was screaming and eventually hoarse. Finally, I had to hang up as I was waiting for Clooney to call. This was before caller ID and call waiting. So I hung up and called Clooney's number, and his assistant told me he just ran to get a Coke and would call back. She too had a soft voice and commented on mine. I explained that years of smoking had to have contributed to it. Then I told her about being on the phone yelling at Steiger.

A few minutes later, Steiger calls back and is just rambling random, nutty things. I cut him off with, "Mr. Steiger, I really can't talk. I promise I'll call back, but I have another call to take." He keeps going, and just as I am really frustrated, Clooney cracks up and says, "It's me, George."

Stephen Whitty, *Star-Ledger*

It's not funny, but the oddest thing was when Angelina Jolie looked down at a folder I had with me on which I'd written her name. Apparently my handwriting is a lot like her father's, with whom she's on difficult terms at best, and it visibly spooked her; she thought I'd gotten it from him before our meeting.

Rob Salem, *Toronto Star*

Not counting drunken misadventures (either me or the talent or both), there was the time I was interviewing Craig T. Nelson and

Jobeth Williams for *Poltergeist II*, when a rope suddenly snaked down outside the hotel room window, recalling a scene from the first movie (I'm guessing window washers, though we never did find out).

"If that's Zelda (Rubinstein, the small medium) on the other end, I'm outta here," deadpanned Nelson.

Okay, so it doesn't read all that funny. You had to be there.

Dave Walker, *New Orleans Times-Picayune*

Nothing much comes to mind. I'm seldom in a situation where I'm with someone in an unguarded moment, and don't really seek that out. The conversation is a transaction, and participants on both ends know it. That said, I was interviewing Paul Maguire, the NBC football announcer, once in his hotel lobby the morning after a game. His eyes were red and he was drinking a Budweiser. It was about 10 A.M. He was great, though obviously hung over. About six questions in, he stopped and said, "Are you writing a book?" The interview was over. I got what I needed, but I've always loved the way he announced he was done talking. It wasn't rude, just succinct, and we both laughed about it.

Tim Riley, *Woodland Daily Democrat*

I was hoping for a wardrobe malfunction when talking to Raquel Welch, but it never happened.

Hanh Nguyen, TVGuide.com

I have loved Leslie Nielsen because of the two sides of his career: dramatic (such as in *Tammy and the Bachelor*) and comedic (*Airplane* and other slapstick comedies). In the middle of an interview for one of the *Scary Movie* films, he had the most perfect deadpan delivery for his answers as he used a fart machine repeatedly to punctuate his pauses.

Margie Barron, *Production Update*

For a Travel Channel special, there was a satellite interview with the King of Jordan. I asked him, "Is it good to be king?" He laughed.

12

Memorable Moments

Some interviews are forgettable; you don't give them a second thought. But some interviews are so memorable, they stay with you for life. At least they do for me. Sometimes an interview, whether it is a one-on-one, a roundtable, or a phoner, has a special place in my memories.

My interview with Chris Lemmon ranks among my all-time favorite interviews, because he opened up about his father, legendary actor Jack Lemmon, and the rest of his family. Chris adored his father and was eager to talk about his recently released biography of their lives. He related many funny stories, but my favorite was Jack's final joke. After Jack had passed away, Chris walked to the site where Jack was buried and read the epitaph for the first time: "Jack Lemmon in . . ." Chris laughed, looked up to the sky, and said, "Pop, you did it to me again." It was evident how much Chris adored his father and his own family.

Chris Lawford was a memorable interview for many reasons. He comes from a prominent family (he is the son of actor Peter Lawford and Pat Kennedy), and he has an interesting and diverse educational background (J.D. at Boston College, M.A. in Clinical Psychology from Harvard Medical School). But it was his personal feelings about Hollywood that stuck with me the most. I interviewed

Chris when the 2005 film, *The World's Fastest Indian,* was released. The interview was scheduled to be 20 minutes, but we ended up talking for well over 45 minutes. Chris compared today's "stars" and those of his father's generation in depth. Peter Lawford and his contemporaries were actors during the old studio days and were able to act, sing, and dance. Many actors now (including Chris, himself) cannot sing or dance. It was fun to hear him describe the differences between old Hollywood and the Hollywood of today.

My conversations with Shirley MacLaine stand out in my mind, as well, because she opened up about her personal beliefs. Yes, we talked about her earlier days in the business, working with Frank Sinatra and Dean Martin, her book writing, her films, her seminars, and her stage work. We also discussed her metaphysical philosophies and belief in extraterrestrial beings. In one interview, she described several different alien cultures and told me that the Vatican knows about the existence of other beings and that she has the internal papers from Monsignor Balducci, the right-hand man to several Popes, to prove it. She is an interesting and intelligent woman, and I enjoyed speaking with her very much. And we both had crushes on Dean Martin!

My interview with up-and-coming country music star Keith Walker was especially memorable because of the format. We didn't do the interview in a studio—we did it in a living room. It was cozier that way and was more appropriate for the electronic press kit he was building. However, because it wasn't done in a professional location, we had to contend with outside noises, like barking dogs and cars zooming by. Each time there was a noise, we had to stop the interview. But then the sound and camera would get going again, and the interview would continue. Despite the interview breaks, it was fun to do this kind of interview, and I enjoyed learning more about this talented guy.

Interviews are especially memorable to me when celebrities get real and dish about their families, talk about their feelings, and hold interviews with interesting formats. My colleagues feel the same. For this chapter, they were asked, "What was your most memorable interview?" Read on.

Candace Havens, FYI Television

Julie Andrews will always be Mary Poppins to me, which is a good thing. I had a chance to talk with her a few years ago about a project, and she was exactly like I'd always dreamed: poised, gracious, and an absolutely lovely human being with a great sense of humor. That was the only time I'd ever been really nervous about an interview. I didn't want her to wreck my idea of who she was, and she didn't.

George Pennacchio, KABC-TV

For me, it's never the big star or the big "get" on a red carpet—it all goes back to Hollywood history. Years ago, Maureen O'Hara was promoting a book, and I was offered an interview with her. When she walked through our newsroom, now a woman in her eighties, I watched the newsroom just stop. I felt it was a rare moment from a time gone by when so many of us felt like we were in the presence of a real "movie star." Maureen couldn't have been more delightful, sharing her life's stories. It was memorable because she was as vibrant and full of life then as she was in her old pictures—many of which she called "stinkers."

I also always love interviewing Phyllis Diller. She was the first person I saw perform "live" as a kid, tagging along with my parents on a night out. Her laugh is priceless, and I have it on camera time and time again. She loves flowers, so when she came to the station one day to talk, people in our newsroom grabbed roses and handed them to her one by one as she made her way to where we'd do the interview. When she got there, we had a nice vase with water already in it for her to place the roses—which we then kept in the shot. Over the years, my wife and I have become good friends of Phyllis, and we have also become avid collectors of her art.

Alex Strachan, *Postmedia News*

Too many to name. Jeremy Irons, certainly. Big cat experts from South Africa I had lunch with at a recent TCA gathering, but that was for reasons of personal interest. I did a phone interview with Michael Palin that I really enjoyed, shortly after he did his *Sahara with Michael Palin* series for the BBC, and I was about to head into the Namibian desert myself.

Anderson Cooper was, and still is, one of my favorites. I talked to him a number of years back when he was doing *The Mole* as a reality TV host. No one else wanted to talk to him, it seemed, so we ended up BS-ing at a TCA get-together at the Huntington Library in Pasadena for more than an hour. We really got into it, in a conversational piece about Africa, politics, the changing shape of TV news, and how he wanted to get back into TV news but didn't like the way network newscasts were going. Less than six months later, he was on CNN, 9/11 happened, and we all know the rest. I've never forgotten that conversation; it was a career highlight for me. It's in the memory bank, anyway.

Winnie Bonelli, North Jersey Media Group

There have been many, but maybe George Clooney because he refuses to take himself too seriously and doesn't buy into the whole star status thing.

David Sheehan, Hollywood Close-Ups, Inc.

I think it was Paul Newman. I had talked with him back in the '70s on the set of *Towering Inferno*, then again many times during the '80s and '90s and early 2000s. But it was the one sit-down at the Charlotte Speedway talking about *Cars* in 2008 or so when it all came together. Paul had a chance to look back at his life on-screen and with the charity products to do some summing up, some nostalgia, and some "what has it all meant."

Stephen Whitty, *Star-Ledger*

Peter O'Toole had to reschedule what would have been a quick interview in his hotel room because he had a sore throat. We ended up having a long one several days later in the Oak Bar of the Plaza Hotel over pints of Guinness. That will always be a high point.

Hanh Nguyen, TVGuide.com

In person, I have to say that Julie Andrews is everything you want her to be—elegant, gorgeous, charming, and such a foul-mouthed broad. During an interview for *The Princess Diaries*, I impressed her with my knowledge of English history to the point that she did a double-take and asked me how I knew that bit of trivia. Later, she complimented my name. Mary Poppins likes my name!

On the phone, I'd say voice actor Peter Cullen fulfilled all my geek fantasies. He was appreciative that I was a true fan of his work, and as a bonus, he recorded an outgoing voicemail for me and my two brothers . . . in the voice of Optimus Prime from *The Transformers*.

Rob Salem, *Toronto Star*

Sean Connery, my hero. It was the junket for *Rising Sun* (which he also produced), and he was in a particularly pissy mood, since the Japanese were all over him about the movie's depiction of their business ethics.

I was terrified—if you've ever read an interview with Sean Connery, you know he eats journalists for breakfast. Plus it was an early-morning roundtable, and I had stupidly decided to pick the night before to hit every seedy bar in New York. I had gotten back to the hotel maybe half an hour before.

Connery stalked to our table with a black cloud hovering over his head. I had nothing. Then I noticed the tattoos up and down both arms. I mean, how many times have we seen this man without a shirt? Who knew?

Not able to form an entire sentence, I just pointed and said, "Tattoo." Connery glared at me for what seemed like an hour, then leaned into my face and said, "No, I did not wake up one morning hung-over next to an ugly hooker."

I still wasn't sure if he liked me or was about to snap my head off and shove it down into my neck hole. Turns out it was the former, and the rest of the session it was just him and me, ignoring the others at the table, mostly talking tattoos . . . "Thish one's a thistle, thish faded one says 'Scotland Forever,' thish one I got in the Merchant Marine."

Rob Owen, *Pittsburgh Post-Gazette*

The interviews I enjoy most are the ones when the people I am interviewing surprise me with their wit and intelligence. I did some interviews last summer with Carrie Brownstein from *Portlandia*. She was just so smart, and that I found very refreshing because her answers didn't sound canned. A lot of times, I think, celebrities are trained to give canned answers. So when you find someone who doesn't do that, it's fantastic.

Jacqueline Cutler, Tribune Media Services

Gloria Steinem in her home. She politicized me when I was 14. I became a proud feminist and have reared two feminists, one of whom is a boy.

Valerie Milano, *Hollywood Today*

Donald Trump, and I kept trying to get closer to see if his hair really is real.

Dave Walker, *New Orleans Times-Picayune*

When this question comes up, I recall very vague memories of talking to George Lucas. I think this was on my first TV tour, not long after getting my first TV columnist job, and he was promoting *Young Indiana Jones*. It was after the Q&A, and he was standing and talking to just a few other reporters. I worked my way in. This was between the *Star Wars* trilogies. This was the guy who'd made *American Graffiti* (the first movie I ever sat through twice in a row), *Raiders*, and the *Star Wars* movies. I remember thinking, "This job is going to be pretty cool." And I was right. I could've asked him all of my Boba Fett questions but didn't.

Most of the other personally memorable interviews have been with musicians I admire, ranging from Don Was to Brian Wilson to Mojo Nixon to Max Weinberg. And, for a story, I once got to play in the VH1 Fairway to Heaven golf tournament on the same team as Bobby Keyes, the Rolling Stones sax player and hell-raiser. He and Keith Richards once threw a TV set out of a Denver hotel window, which I've always believed was the purest expression of television criticism.

Julio Martinez, *VIP Latino Magazine*, KPFK Radio

In 1996, I interviewed Natasha Richardson and Liam Neeson by phone regarding their experience of providing the voices of historic figures from the PBS series, *The Great War and the Shaping of the 20th Century*. They were each on separate house phones from their apartment on the East Coast. They were not only exceedingly gracious, but they also read some of their favorite quotes from the script. After half an hour, I had more info than I could ever use. At the end, Richardson offered, "If you find you need more, please ring back." When I hung up the phone, I felt like I was glowing.

Gerri Miller, Freelance

Hard to say—I've literally done thousands, and they blend together after a while!

Brian Sebastian, Movie Reviews & More

Oprah Winfrey and Coretta Scott King. I was not supposed to get these two interviews. Oprah I got in the parking lot by myself in between her security detail. For Coretta Scott King, I ran from one hotel to another to get a TV slot that I was not supposed to have.

Scott Pierce, *Salt Lake Tribune*

This is such a hard question. If I had to pick one, it would probably be a one-on-one I did with Maureen O'Hara. She was incredibly charming, and I have been a fan all my life. Or at least since I saw *Miracle on 34th Street* and *The Parent Trap*.

Michael Lee, RadioFree.com

I could actually list quite a few for a litany of different reasons. Some are memorable for being funny, some for being enlightening, some for being a chance to meet an idol. I've had a handful of experiences where the talent has not only thanked me at the end of the interview but has also taken a moment to talk about why the experience was better than their typical experience with reporters. I've always felt a certain sense of pride on those occasions, because someone familiar with the business is going out of their way to compliment you for something that outsiders may feel is completely generic and interchangeable. That's the long, corny, sentimental answer to the question. The blunt answer is, "Teresa Palmer. Because we talked about dogs, and I got hugs— from Teresa Palmer."

Fred Topel, Crave Online

Sitting in Arnold Schwarzenegger's trailer on the set of *Terminator 3*. Arnold was my favorite growing up and of course the Terminator movies were huge. To be on the set with him, in his personal trailer, asking him questions and getting really in depth, I felt like I'd made it.

Rick Bentley, *Fresno Bee*

There are so many that it's hard to pick just one. So, I'll just go with my first. I had the chance to visit the set of *Stripes* when it was filming and talk with Sean Young. I'm sure it was an awful interview on my part, but it will always remain meaningful because it was when I stopped being an entertainment virgin.

Mike Reynolds, Veteran Entertainment Journalist

A world-famous pop group had refused to do any interviews for some time and at the MIDEM (French music festival) marketplace in Cannes, one January, I somehow hooked up with someone who got me an interview with these famed but recently reclusive stars. A music publisher friend of mine was a photo nut and always had his camera with him. He suggested that it might be great if he came along and took some shots. Not being open to having anyone else in the room, I was reluctant but for some reason relented and said, "Okay." I gave him the hotel room number and time to meet, and he assured me he would be there. When I arrived, he was not to be found; I was somewhat relieved.

The introduction to each member of the superstar group was polite but not overwhelmingly friendly. One member asked if I had a photographer. I was surprised at the question but relieved that my friend had been so insightful in his offer. I told them he was on his way. The group arranged themselves in a way my microphones could pick all of them up and we began. But after the first question, another group member asked when the photographer would arrive. For about seven minutes, it was one question, a non-answer back, and then a "Where's the photographer?" or "Are you sure there's a photographer coming?" Suddenly, a knock on the door. My friend had arrived, camera in hand and an apology at the ready for being late.

The group members were up and out on the balcony, ushering me to join them. (Something I hate to do with celebrities is have my photo taken with them.) All was fine during the longer-than-expected photo shoot, but once it was over, it was "Thanks very much, great to see you," and off they went! Interview over. I guess they just wanted photos showing they were being press-friendly again!

Howard Benjamin, Interview Factory Radio Networks

This has to be Roy Orbison. What a gentle spirit and a truly gifted performer and songwriter. I met him at his home in the Malibu colony, and I was armed with more information about his life than the FBI could have compiled. He was genuinely impressed by the research and kept saying, "How do you know that?" I said, "It's my job." He had a number of interviews to do that day, so my time with him was limited. When we finished, he said, "I can hardly wait until we can do this again." At the end of the interview, I always give the performer my business card and say, "Call anytime for any reason." Several years later he did call and said he had been working on a project with Bob Dylan, George Harrison, Tom Petty, and Jeff Lynne (The Traveling Wilburys), and he was looking forward to seeing me again to talk about it. He died a few weeks later. The world is an empty place without that soaring voice.

Donna Plesh, Thecolumnists.com

Walter Cronkite. Wow. I was a young journalist who had grown up watching him on the *CBS Evening News*. Then I had an opportunity to interview him. What I remember most is that he was a great interview, and he patiently answered every question I asked, even though I am positive he had answered the same questions a million times or more.

Tim Riley, *Woodland Daily Democrat*

Interviewing Roger Moore late at night in San Francisco during the filming of the James Bond film, *A View to a Kill*. It was only memorable because I am a big fan of the Bond films and found Roger Moore very charming and pleasant, and in keeping with the character he played on TV in *The Saint*.

Margie Barron, *Production Update*

Bob Hope, at his home in Toluca Lake. I had interviewed Bob Hope a few times before, but this was after he turned 90, and although still very sharp, his hearing was very bad. His daughter Linda put a microphone in front of me and put earphones on Bob so he could just hear my voice without any outside sounds. I learned quickly not to joke around with Bob. He was a very serious person when doing interviews.

13

Location, Location, Location

While many of my colleagues have been in somewhat strange locations for interviews, I have not been so lucky. Actually, the most unusual place I have conducted an interview was the Santa Monica Pier. I had arranged to meet director David R. Ellis there to interview him for a feature article for a local newspaper. He lived in Malibu, and I lived further south. He suggested that we meet at the pier, because he had filmed his latest movie, *Cellular,* there. So, we sat on a bench at the pier for the interview. With the noise of the activities on the pier as well as the whipping wind, the location was not the most ideal. It was, however, very picturesque.

I also met Paul Petersen at a local coffee house, where we spent over an hour talking about his career, life, and A Minor Consideration—his organization that protects the interests of young actors and all child workers. Petersen grew up in front of the camera, having been in *The Donna Reed Show* from 1958–1966. He also appeared in several feature films, made-for-TV movies, and other television shows. He has had an interesting life. He worked as a chauffeur for a while and has written books. This brought me to ask if he would ever write his autobiography. "I won't do it," was his reply. "I won't because I am a published author, and I want a good finish. And the only good finish for me, given this mission, is the day we pass national legislation that ends the exemption to child labor laws suffered by kids in entertainment—the kids who pick our food, who deliver door-to-door, who are selling flowers on street corners. When that day comes, then I'll have a reason to say, 'What I've set for myself has been accomplished.'"

"How are we going to get Hollywood to help us change the rules?" I asked.

"You can accomplish anything in Hollywood if you make sure everybody gets to take a bow. And that's what I do."

Interviewing actors on set is often challenging, but I thoroughly enjoyed the press day I spent on the set of *Ruby and the Rockits* (a TV show on ABC Family for one season) with the Cassidy Brothers. When they were between blocking and rehearsing scenes, they came over to talk with our press group, which numbered about ten of us. Shaun, David, and Patrick all spoke with us on the set, but we managed to snag Ryan during lunch, and he was great fun. When people are eating, they are less inhibited and friendlier.

Speaking of eating, at an evening dinner event during one TCA Press Tour, I noticed Tim Daly sitting alone at a table. He had his dinner in front of him; but hey, this was a press event. So I asked if I could sit with him. He was friendly and said yes. We had a delightful dinner, during which he told me several stories about his career and life. Although it was not the optimum place or time, it was the only chance I had to get him alone, and I took it.

For this chapter, my colleagues were asked, "Where is the most interesting place you have conducted an interview?" As you read the following pages, you'll find that some of my colleagues have been to some pretty outrageous locations for interviews: bedrooms, private planes, exotic locations, etc. And all I have in my repertoire are sets, a coffee house, and that darn Santa Monica Pier!

Alex Strachan, *Postmedia News*

There have been too many to name. But I would have to say in Africa once, while on holiday. It was a tough one to write afterwards, because once you're back home, you don't have the in-the-moment setting to inspire you. Good interview, but I was never really happy with the piece that emerged at the end. I always felt it was missing something.

George Pennacchio, KABC-TV

Once, I wanted to interview Tom Selleck when he was guest-starring on *Boston Legal,* but I couldn't get on the set. So I called Tom's publicist and explained that I'd really like to talk to him about his arc on the show and other items of interest. Well, Tom said he'd do the interview, and it so happened he was going to be in the area near where I live a day or two later. So Tom Selleck came to my house and did the interview in my family room. He's a nice man and a class act.

Howard Benjamin, Interview Factory Radio Networks

Over the years I've cornered people in public restrooms and have even used my car in a pinch. But what has to be the strangest place happened not once, not twice, but three times in my career. It was in bed. The first time it was a rough-and-tumble female country singer named Gus Hardin. She insisted that she did her best thinking in bed, so that's where the interview took place.

The second time was with—are you sensing a trend here?—one of the true queens of country music, Miss Dotty West. Strangely enough, it was at the very same hotel where I spoke to Gus Hardin. She said she was a little under the weather that day and would prefer to tell her story while in bed. It seemed like a perfectly normal request to me, so I agreed.

The third, and now here's where it gets a little kinky, was with the songwriting superstar duo, Cynthia Weil and her husband Barry Mann. She had suffered a back injury the day before the interview, and being the trooper that she is, she wanted to go through with the interview anyway. So there all three of us laid, laughing, reminiscing, and talking about the inspiration for more than a dozen Top Ten songs. Combined, they have written and published 635 tunes and have created one of the most enviable music catalogues in the history of popular music.

Mike Reynolds, Veteran Entertainment Journalist

A female had written a book about her life. She was married, and I knew her husband—not very well, but I knew him. I went to the house and knocked on the door. No answer. It took four different attempts before the door opened and a rather bedraggled author appeared, wearing a very short see-through slip and nothing underneath! She invited me into the house and asked where I wanted to set up and do the interview. I told her that as long as she was comfortable, we could do it anywhere. "Well, I've been in bed, so let's do it there."

How could I refuse?

I set up the recording equipment, took off my shoes, and jumped into bed with the virtually naked author.

We had been talking for about 40 minutes when the bedroom door opened and in walked her husband. "Oh, hi, Mike! Hello dear! Sorry to disturb you, I'll let you carry on. Good to see you, Mike." Why was I breaking into a sweat?

Rick Bentley, *Fresno Bee*

It may not be the most interesting, but the ones that stick in my mind are those conducted at restaurants. These are noisy places where people are stuffing food in their mouths. Not a perfect location to talk.

The weirdest restaurant interview was at the Hard Rock Cafe in New Orleans. Anthony Michael Hall was in town to talk about *Johnny Be Good,* and the club was the location. Not only was it impossible to hear his answers, Hall left the table multiple times to visit the restroom. He finally left and never came back.

Rob Owen, *Pittsburgh Post-Gazette*

When TNT did the *Babylon Five* spin-off series *Crusade*, I had the idea that I wanted to go on the set and get made up as an alien so I could write a story about what it's like to have all that makeup put on you, how long it takes, and that sort of thing. Well, the show was over budget, and it turned out to be the final episode before it got cancelled—before they were even through their production order. So they had no aliens that required makeup that episode. It was crew members who had been turned into zombies. So I said I'd do it. So they put me in a uniform that the people on that spaceship wore, and I was a zombie crew member. And I also needed to interview J. Michael Straczynski, the creator of the show. So, I was sitting there in his office interviewing him while wearing a uniform from his show, which felt very dorky. That was an unusual situation.

Fred Topel, Crave Online

That would have to be Arnold Schwarzenegger's trailer!

Gerri Miller, Freelance

In Bon Jovi's private plane between L.A. and Red Rocks in Colorado.

Michael Lee, RadioFree.com

Did I mention the women's locker room?

Candace Havens, FYI Television

A NASCAR race. I don't recommend it.

Julio Martinez, *VIP Latino Magazine*, KPFK Radio

In 1984, I interviewed a musician on the Orkney Islands, north of the mainland of Scotland. We were standing in the middle of the massive Neolithic stone formation known as the Ring of Brodgar.

Margie Barron, *Production Update*

I've done a lot of interviews in hallways. George Lucas gave me a great exclusive interview in a hallway. I caught Ron Howard by the espresso machine off a hotel lobby. But my favorite was when I interviewed Dean Cain on the on-deck circle at Dodger Stadium, and we got into a philosophical discussion and talked about how life was a lot like baseball.

Winnie Bonelli, North Jersey Media Group

Interviewing Jon Bon Jovi in the middle of the field at Giants Stadium in the middle of winter for a British TV special.

There were dozens of interviews in the dressing rooms at the Meadowlands Arena with the likes of KISS, Pink Floyd, Bono, etc.

Tim Riley, *Woodland Daily Democrat*

On the set of *Mr. Belvedere*, when I interviewed Bob Uecker, which I did only because I enjoy baseball and was more interested in his athletic and sports announcing career.

Brian Sebastian, Movie Reviews & More

Between two cars, in a bathroom, and in the middle of an orgy! No really, I can't tell you who.

Jacqueline Cutler, Tribune Media Services

I interviewed nature photographer and wildlife documentarian Dereck Joubert while hanging out of a jeep in Kenya in the middle of the wildebeest migration last fall. Lions, crocs, and zebras were around us.

Valerie Milano, *Hollywood Today*

I interviewed Christiane Amanpour in the Ritz Carlton bathroom in Pasadena.

Stephen Whitty, *Star-Ledger*

It's all mostly done in hotel rooms and publicists' offices, I'm afraid; or if the person is in a real rush, in the back seat of a car on the way to the airport, which is how I spoke to Matt Damon once. It's rarely done in a very memorable setting.

Rob Salem, *Toronto Star*

I have used an adjacent urinal next to Tom Hanks, Patrick Swayze, and Willem Dafoe. I guess I pee a lot. Not much in the way of conversation—these things are invariably awkward, no matter who you stand next to. I did, however, sneak enough of a sideways peek to confirm the rumors about a certain actor's large penis.

Dave Walker, *New Orleans Times-Picayune*

I've been to *24*'s CTU set, the *Studio 60 on the Sunset Strip* set, *Friends* set, *ER* set, etc. A lot of them. I was interviewing Darrell Hammond of *Saturday Night Live* once in the audience seats at 8H and had seen Phil Hartman do a great guest spot the night before on Letterman. The episode was going to air that night, and Hammond interrupted a rehearsal to tell Hartman what I'd said. That was pretty cool.

14

Anecdotes

I usually wear a special ring when I go to interviews. It was my grandmother's. It's a conversation piece, because it spins. It's also good luck. Kevin Spacey held my hand and played with my ring during an interview. I had no complaints (it was Kevin Spacey!), but I wasn't able to take any notes during the interview, because he was holding my hand. The ring also caused Rupert Everett to stop an interview for *Shrek 2* to say he was getting hypnotized by my ring. Vince Vaughn also had an eye on my ring, as have many others. As a matter of fact, my ring actually made it into the transcript of the November 2004 roundtable for the film, *Beyond the Sea:*

> Q: How hard was it for you as a director and the star to jump in and out of character? The other actors were saying that you weren't Bobby Darin when you were directing.
>
> Kevin Spacey: It's just part of my character. I'm able to compartmentalize very well and do that (snaps fingers), and I'm out of it, in it. But it was also interesting. It takes a while for actors to start to feel safe and trusting. You ask them to go places that are wildly comic, and they are not quite sure who they're playing, yet. I

remember Greta when we were shooting a scene the first or second night. It was freezing cold, and we were outside in Berlin, and she said [looks at Francine's ring]—*That's the most fascinating ring I've ever seen. It's going to actually hypnotize me.*

My ring also made it into the transcript for the *Shrek 2* roundtable with Rupert Everett.

Q: Do you know what the producers saw in you for Prince Charming? They say confidence, a little bit of arrogance.

Rupert Everett: Really. They don't know me. I was very surprised. [He notices Francine's weird moving ring, and we talk about it hypnotizing him.] No. I was pleased that they wanted me, and you don't ask any questions after that. You might get a nasty answer. Just take it and run.

At least I am remembered by actors, if not for my questions then for my ring!

We all have some anecdotes from our work, and the entertainment business provides us with some pretty interesting ones, to put it mildly. Read on to find out what journalists said when they were asked the question, "What are your most interesting anecdotes?"

Jacqueline Cutler, Tribune Media Services

Pete Seeger, Wynston Marsalis, and others have sung to me. Also, I interviewed Antonio Banderas in his dressing room when he was on Broadway. I am usually a very cool interviewer, but that man is just so damned sexy. I was sitting there, prim, in my knee-length skirt with my *New York Times* in sections, folded, on my lap. During the course of the interview, I managed to drop each section of the newspaper, my purse, my pad, and my pen. He laughed, and I finally said, "Nothing else can fall. Nothing left."

Michael Lee, RadioFree.com

To me, the fun moments have been the opportunities for unique experiences. I've also loved the opportunity to meet talent behind the camera, like animators who created shows from my childhood. Some random moments of fun that immediately come to mind are a dining-in-the-dark experience for *30 Days of Night*; video games, pizza, and a Donkey Kong competition (which I happened to win) for *The King of Kong: A Fistful of Quarters*; attending a drift racing exhibition for *The Fast and the Furious: Tokyo Drift*; playing in a poker tournament in Las Vegas for *The Hangover*; visiting New York for *King Kong*; taking tours of the animation studios at Disney throughout the years; participating in a police training simulation for *Street Kings*; watching a demonstration of live fight choreography for *Ultraviolet*; and catching a roller derby match for *Whip It*. I've also always loved meeting the four-legged critters of film and television, like dogs from *Marley and Me* and *Hotel for Dogs* and a horse from *Secretariat*.

Dave Walker, *New Orleans Times-Picayune*

The *Mad Men* premiere party was at the Beverly Hills Friars' Club, and another critic and I found ourselves checking out memorabilia in some off-limits rooms. Our eyes met, and I knew we felt the same thing. We're about the same age and grew up worshipping the comics who once hung out in the club, which has since been demolished. I wrote the next day that that was about as holy as I ever got to feel. That's not much, but maybe the most meaningful to me.

Aaron Barnhart, *Kansas City Star*

Conan O'Brien is my favorite late-night personality. He makes me laugh as no one else does. He is also my favorite interview. I've interviewed him at least a dozen times over the years, and he is generous with his time and thoughtful with his answers. He has granted me several exclusives. And all because, basically, I'm an unabashed fan of his and can do it while also being a professional in writing about his career. I wish I had more relationships with television people like the one with O'Brien and his right-hand man, Jeff Ross, but they are unique in the business. It is not only rewarding to cover his career, but fun.

Brian Sebastian, Movie Reviews & More

I did an interview at a swing club with a celebrity and had the best time ever with the answers. Yes, we are still friends today!

Tim Riley, *Woodland Daily Democrat*

The best times have always occurred on the TCA Press Tours. I think having lunch on the field of Dodger Stadium rates high on my list. It was also great when former President Ford came to the PBS lunch session. How often does that happen?

Winnie Bonelli, North Jersey Media Group

There have been tons of them, but like any other job you're always concentrating on the current or future assignment. What has been the most gratifying part is the human element when you know that you've truly connected with someone—when there's a bond of trust, where the subjects can share their true feelings, fears, and frustrations, and they know you won't betray them, especially in this era of gossip tabloids.

Howard Benjamin, Interview Factory Radio Networks

I was invited to a Paul McCartney and Wings press conference by a fellow journalist. She had formed a relationship with Paul and Linda McCartney, so she was asked to make up the guest list for the press conference. She said to me, "This is all about the tour and their vegetarian food line, so no Beatles questions."

I'm one that loves a challenge, so during the questions and answers I asked of Paul, "What song are you the most proud of writing?" He answered, "Yesterday." Daggers flew from her eyes! He went on to explain that he woke up with the melody in his head and was sure it was something he had heard from another artist. He questioned everyone he knew if the melody sounded familiar and when they all answered no, he knew that it was an original tune.

It took him months to finish the song that he initially named "Scrambled Eggs." Well, after the press conference was over this colleague raced over to me and said, "How dare you." I said, "He could have picked any of the songs the band sang on tour. How was I to know he'd pick a Beatles song?" She swore that this wasn't the end of it. A few weeks later, I was listening to one of her shows on the radio, and lo and behold, she used the story on "Yesterday" in a Beatles segment. I called her up and told her she owed me an "excerpt" fee for the use of my question and Paul's answer. At that point all we could do was laugh about it. By the way, she never paid me a dime.

Mike Reynolds, Veteran Entertainment Journalist

There were times when TV networks would give me a hotel room for days and just send in one celebrity after another. They would also ensure you had plenty to eat and drink. Most celebrities who came in would need no introduction, and we would be given a list of who we might expect every day so research could be done beforehand.

The day was going well. Another interview done, and I waited for the next celebrity to walk in. A woman walked in on her own and sat down, but I didn't recognize her, so I didn't put the mic on her. She asked where I wanted to put the mic, so I knew she was someone in a show and went ahead, turned on the machine, and then . . . *Hmm! What do I ask?* I didn't know who she was or what show she was on. I began with some general questions, hoping to get a clue. How did she get the show? What made her decide on TV? Finally, after half a dozen questions, I realized who she was. This once-famous actor had been out of the business for some time, and the facial surgery she had just undergone made her unrecognizable. After that, everything went fine.

Rob Owen, *Pittsburgh Post-Gazette*

I remember interviewing Mister Rogers in his office in Pittsburgh when he gave us the exclusive that he was ending *Mister Rogers' Neighborhood*. This would have been, I think, in 1999. We were sitting on a couch in his office, and he put the Daniel striped tiger puppet on his hand. He started having Daniel talk to me. So Daniel was talking to me and, rather than looking at Mister Rogers, I looked at Daniel the puppet and started talking to Daniel. And he commented that that was unusual because most people wouldn't look at the puppet. But I assume because I had grown up on *Neighborhood,* and Daniel was always my favorite character, it was sort of instinctive that I would talk to Daniel and not to Mister Rogers.

Candace Havens, FYI Television

Years ago, the summer I turned 16, I was a dancer on the film, *Urban Cowboy.* John Travolta was talking to some people in a group next to me. I was a kid, and it was John Travolta, so I was basically staring at him. He smiled and told me I had pretty eyes. Flash forward twenty years, and I'm interviewing him for a film. I've talked to him a lot over the years but never had the courage to bring up what happened on *Urban Cowboy.* I finally did, and he told me I still had pretty eyes. I love that guy.

Scott Pierce, *Salt Lake Tribune*

Before she starred in *Sex and the City*, Sarah Jessica Parker—who I had interviewed several times—was being pestered by a critic about comments she had made in the press about wanting to have a baby with boyfriend Robert Downey, Jr. She tried to deflect the questions—having rather publicly broken up with Downey some months earlier—but this guy was persistent. Parker eventually pointed to me, said to the persistent critic, "Ask him. He'll explain it to you," and walked swiftly away.

Gerri Miller, Freelance

Some of the best memories are from the '80s and early '90s, when I was the editor of *Metal Edge* magazine and did a lot of traveling to cover concerts and interview bands, domestically and in Europe (UK, Denmark, etc.), Mexico, and Canada. Some of the more memorable ones included seeing Def Leppard in London, Aerosmith everywhere from Toronto to the private concert opening of L.A.'s House of Blues, and Bon Jovi at Meadowlands Stadium (NJ) and Red Rocks in Colorado. Another cool moment was having Whitesnake's David Coverdale say "hi" to me from the stage during a show at the Nassau Coliseum.

David Sheehan, Hollywood Close-Ups, Inc.

Funniest to me was when I invited some friends and Shirley MacLaine and Marlon Brando to my Mulholland bungalow for a dinner party and to watch one of my shows on the air that night. Marlon came to the back door in jeans and a sweatshirt, and the cook in the kitchen thought he was a delivery man. So he pretended to be one for a few laughs.

Hanh Nguyen, TVGuide.com

Syfy had a junket in Florida during which I experienced the highs and lows of theme parks. I am a huge chicken when it comes to horror films. I never ever watch them, mainly because my imagination really responds to visuals, and it's when I go to bed at night that all of that input from the movie gets overlaid on the darkness. Not good. Anyway, for one night Syfy got the reporters an express pass through all of its haunted houses, which meant we got to jump the line and get back-to-back, concentrated scares. I literally clung to the poor girl in front of me the entire time and kept my eyes on the floor through all eight houses. The next day, the Wizarding World of Harry Potter theme park was closed off just for our use, and I rode one particular rollercoaster several times in a row with *Top Chef* contestant Marcel Vigneron. Such a surreal work trip!

Julio Martinez, *VIP Latino Magazine*, KPFK Radio

In 2001, I had an appointment to interview Salma Hayek, during the TCA Press Tour being held at the Ritz Carlton in Pasadena, about her role as producer/star of the Showtime film, *In the Time of the Butterflies*. When she found out I was writing for a Latino publication, she said, "Let's walk in the rose garden." During the interview, she asked about my background, and I told her that my parents had been professional Latin ballroom dancers during the late '30s and early '40s. She asked if I could dance, and then we did an impromptu rhumba in the middle of the roses. That was fun.

15

Swag

Swag. What is it? Simply put, swag is a freebie. I don't know any journalists who would be swayed by swag. Some outlets won't allow their writers to accept free items, and the rest of us have journalistic integrity. But we do work hard, and I personally feel it's okay to accept a gift once in a while. It's not going to influence my article, and it is fun to get things that are unexpected, so why not? I've got common swag, cool swag, interesting swag, and even spectacular swag. I might not always keep it, but it's always fun to receive.

Take a look around my house, and you'll find a lot of swag items. Baseball caps, T-shirts, books, and CDs are everywhere. Coffee mugs are also common swag. TV networks are more likely to send coffee mugs than movie studios. At the TCA Press Tour one year, when Charles Gibson first became the host of *ABC World News,* I was talking to the producer of the show about the story I was writing on Mr. Gibson. The producer asked me if I had received one of the new coffee mugs, and I said "yes." He then proceeded to give me several more, telling me that I might as well have an entire set. Schlepping them around with me all day was a chore, but they are great mugs!

One of the coolest pieces of swag I have been given is a pair of Puma shoes. I received an invitation to a movie press event, and attached to it was a note to supply my shoe size with my RSVP. At the movie event, I was handed a pair of cool, comfortable Puma shoes that I am wearing as I write this chapter. I have received countless comments about the shoes. They are, in a word, awesome.

In addition to the traditional and the cool, I have received a wide variety of interesting swag. I like curling up in the incredibly warm blanket sent to me from Paramount/DreamWorks for their 2010 movie, *How to Train Your Dragon.* I enjoy looking at the countless Disney statuettes I've received, such as a statue of Tinker Bell (for attending an event at Disneyland); a glass slipper (for the DVD release of *Twice Charmed*); a telephone (from a press junket for *The Incredibles*); a Jiminy Cricket figurine; and a Pinocchio marionette. I enjoy using the clock from Columbia/TriStar Home Entertainment and several kitchen utensils, including a timer, from Fox's *Kitchen Nightmares.* I have pillows, picture frames, and bags of all shapes and sizes scattered around the house.

Once in a while, something pretty spectacular comes my way. I was given roundtrip airline tickets courtesy of the 2004 film, *Beyond the Sea.* Another time, for the 2007 film *License to Wed,* we were given several nights at a Sandals Resort.

Without a doubt, these are pretty cool gifts. But if you think all these things are great, you should be a celebrity! Those folks get thousands of dollars of swag all the time. For presenting at an awards show, they receive incredible (and incredibly expensive) swag, such as jewelry, spa vacations, and merchandise of all kinds. I ask you, is that fair? Why not disperse those sparkling goodies to the press, who give the celebs their media attention in the first place? If anyone from a studio is reading this, I could use a new bicycle! Of course, I'm just kidding. Or am I?

While I am always grateful for swag, I don't always keep it. A lot of my swag is donated to the Los Angeles Children's Hospital. Having been in the hospital a lot when I was younger, I know what it's like to be stuck in a room surrounded by doctors, nurses, and a lot of needles! So I always feel good about giving the items to the children.

Swag won't sway a credible journalist one way or another. But freebies are a fun perk of the job. Whether we keep them or donate them, we each have swag items that are special to us. In this chapter, journalists answer the question, "What is the best swag you've ever received?"

Mike Reynolds, Veteran Entertainment Journalist

So many! Like being allowed to select more than 100 rare albums from a record company vault; having a standing order of two cases of wine each week, just for me, from another; being provided full clothing apparel by record companies; and having cars take me to concerts all over the UK.

While still based in London, I visited the offices of a well-known record company. The publicist, who I knew very well, asked what I was doing on a particular day the following week. I said, "Nothing important." "Okay. Be here at 8:30 sharp with your passport!"

I arrive on the agreed date and at the agreed time. A coach is being loaded with wine and beer, and about 11 other journalists are waiting around. We are put on the bus, and as we drive out of London, the wine and beer are flowing! We arrive out in the country at a private airport. As we get into the plane, flight attendants (one for every two journalists) are asking what we would like to drink. The plane takes off, and we are being well looked after.

We land but don't know where and are not told. Guided to a coach, laden with more wine and beer, we set off through a countryside, we know not where. We arrive at some gates guarding a long driveway. At either side of the gates are waiters in tails with trays of wine, champagne, and glasses. We are each given a drink and guided down the driveway into a huge chateau.

Once inside, we are shown into a large hall with a table set for a meal. Music is being played through speakers set in the ceiling.

We are told that we are in France and that a certain British pop star, who lives in Switzerland because of the tax situation, is meeting us halfway between the UK and his home, has a new album out, and would like to introduce us to it. He and his fellow collaborator arrive; we shake hands, sit down and just have a friendly talk about nothing in particular during a meal of several courses. After the meal we have photos taken and are given beautiful briefcases with the album and press materials. We are taken down to the wine cellar and invited to choose two bottles of wine, say goodbye to the artist, and head back to the bus, where the whole drink/travel routine is repeated in reverse. It is early evening when we arrive back in London.

To this day, I still don't know where we went, but it was a very expensive day out for a dozen privileged journalists, and probably the most unusual "swag" we ever received during a crazy swag-laden period when certain people even had their home kitchen remodeling paid for by entertainment companies.

Aaron Barnhart, *Kansas City Star*

I get a large amount of swag every year and give it out in September in a drawing at the annual pilots-watching event I hold for readers.

Alex Strachan, *Postmedia News*

I'm uncomfortable with swag in general—my hard news background again—but I must say, the Directors Guild of America came up with truly wonderful and inspired chachkes a number of years back, when they hosted a DGA function and handed out these tiny, inch-high brass replicas of director's chairs with the critic's name inscribed on the back. Another cute chachka, and one for the grandkids, was a personalized nameplate from a set visit to *The Office*.

I wouldn't say swag has ever influenced one of my reviews, but it does make me a little uncomfortable. The whole idea of "pigs at the trough" and all that. Then again, from what I understand, TCA has nothing on the Hollywood Foreign Press Association when it comes to swag.

The optics are never good, though. And this business is a lot about optics. In hard news, for example, you would never want to be seen getting a free lunch from the cops or a bottle of scotch from a politician you're supposed to be writing about.

Earlier you asked about popular misconceptions of the job. I would add that one big misconception is that somehow TV critics and movie critics can be bought off with swag. It may be true of bloggers, but I definitely wouldn't say that about real journos who work for the working press.

As far as TCA's are concerned, I've always chosen to look at it as being an invited guest to the other guy's birthday party. You're not there to be rude and constantly pick fights by asking overly aggressive questions, but at the same time you don't have to walk out the door with all the party gifts at the end.

Bonnie Siegler, Freelance

One time, in a Golden Globe suite, I received a regular suitcase that I still use today, filled with freebies from the suite that day, including shoes, perfume, gift certificates, and jewelry.

Brian Sebastian, Movie Reviews & More

Airplane tickets from the movie, *Beyond the Sea,* starring Kevin Spacey.

George Pennacchio, KABC-TV

My brother loved getting all the movie T-shirts I passed his way. When people would say about the movie he was advertising on his chest, "Hey, how is that movie?" He'd say, "Oh, I don't know. I didn't see it. This was a gift." I always thought that was funny, but I guess it doesn't answer your question. I think one of the funniest items I ever got was from the movie, *There's Something about Mary*. I opened my mail one day to receive a stuffed animal of a dog in a body cast. I still have it.

Candace Havens, FYI Television

I'm boring in that respect. I love the books and screenplays that are sometimes sent out for various projects. I usually keep those.

Dave Walker, *New Orleans Times-Picayune*

I mostly don't take it and don't keep it when I do. Co-workers and hotel room attendants get it all.

Rob Salem, *Toronto Star*

My *Sammo Hung* inflatable punching bag, which sits in my chair at my desk when I'm not there to fool my editor into thinking that I'm actually in the office.

Stephen Whitty, *Star-Ledger*

I can't, and wouldn't, accept anything valuable. Most of what I get is just silly promotional stuff, and it seems to run in cycles. One year, everybody was sending alarm clocks with their movie's logo on the face. Another year, it was tiny glass globes. I do have a stuffed-animal figure of a dog with the full-body cast from *There's Something About Mary* lying around somewhere. That was pretty cute.

Tim Riley, *Woodland Daily Democrat*

I think I am partial to the *Pan Am* travel bag we received from ABC. I also enjoy getting the baseball caps from the networks. The *Baseball* books from Ken Burns also rate high.

Jacqueline Cutler, Tribune Media Services

I love the robe that was given for a nail salon show last year.

Valerie Milano, *Hollywood Today*

Fox gave me a garment bag, and inside was a *Models Inc.* Polaroid camera.

Winnie Bonelli, North Jersey Media Group

It's not about the most expensive items. It might be a T-shirt for a movie or TV series that a friend or relative enjoys. I'll give you a prime example. For years, I gave all my *American Idol* memorabilia to a neighbor for her niece. Last season, the show sent a TV snack table that I automatically passed along. It turns out that the niece has outgrown her interest in the series, so my neighbor Marge kept it because she and her husband Fred had become devoted viewers of the program. Fred developed pneumonia and was hospitalized. After visiting for a while, Marge was about to leave when she had second thoughts: "Maybe I'll stay with Fred and leave after *American Idol*." In the middle of the telecast, Fred had a heart attack, and they couldn't save him. When I dropped by Marge's the other day, she remarked how much that table meant, and she uses it when she eats alone in front of the TV set.

Sean Daly, *New York Post*

$5000 laser eye surgery, which I never used. And a week-long stay on a private island in Florida—which I also never used. So probably a leather jacket or a cell phone. By the way, do trips to London and Maui and Dubai count?

Donna Plesh, Thecolumnists.com

An autographed copy of John Houseman's book, *Front and Center*. It resides on my bookshelf to this day.

Howard Benjamin, Interview Factory Radio Networks

By far it was at the Television Critics Association meeting in 1994 when the Fox network handed out luggage with a Polaroid camera, a personalized NFL football jersey, and a Mighty Morphin Power Ranger doll all tucked inside. There was another time at TCA where we got cell phones from CNN and state-of-the-art Motorola pagers that were only supposed to work for six months for free and, in fact, went on to provide four years of service at no cost.

Rick Bentley, *Fresno Bee*

I have always worked for companies with strict rules about what swag could be kept. So most of it has been donated to charity.

There are two items very dear to me. One of the great things about this job is the chance to meet people I watched on TV and in films when I was young. I'll never forget sitting down with Clayton Moore to talk about *The Lone Ranger* or having Chuck Connors allow me to hold one of the original rifles from *The Rifleman*.

The two prize possessions are a small Lamb Chop pin sent to me by ventriloquist Shari Lewis after an interview and a Ping-Pong ball given to me by Bob Keeshan, who played Captain Kangaroo. Both were nice connections to my youth.

Michael Lee, RadioFree.com

Jeff Bridges counts photography among his hobbies and has been known to create photo books of pictures he takes from the sets of his movies. He handed out one such book to all the attending press at the junket for *The Door in the Floor* and was gracious enough to autograph them as well. As I mentioned, this happened to be my first official junket, so I was perhaps immediately spoiled by this atypical precedent. Although impressive and diverse swag like bags, T-shirts, souvenirs, lithographs, soundtracks, video games, and toys would follow, none of it would be as thoughtful and personal until Jeff Bridges repeated this act of generosity at the junket for *The Amateurs*, where he once again handed out photo books he had created for that film experience.

Gerri Miller, Freelance

I've received everything from clothes and jewelry to cosmetics, grooming services, and electronics like an iPod and cameras.

Julio Martinez, *VIP Latino Magazine*, KPFK Radio

I received the complete *Sex in the City* DVD set. It made me so happy to see how happy it made my eighteen-year-old daughter when I gave it to her.

Fred Topel, Crave Online

I still use the notebook from *The Notebook* today—although I am on my second notebook. Luckily, I had an extra one.

Hanh Nguyen, TVGuide.com

I don't tend to get ridiculously expensive swag since it's against policy, but among some of the oddest (and therefore best because they tickled me so much) swag I've received are a Breathalyzer and three pairs of thong panties (new and unused, of course!).

Rob Owen, *Pittsburgh Post-Gazette*

Probably the framed *Battlestar Galactica* "Last Supper" picture. I like that one a lot. I've got that one hanging up in the house. I just thought that was a nice, creative move. There's a lot less swag than there used to be, and much of it gets put on the freebie table or given to friends for charity auctions.

16

Final Thoughts

When you are an entertainment journalist, you learn on the job. It's sink or swim, and you have to be willing to tread water without a life preserver nearby. But once you get the hang of working with celebrities and their publicists, you'll have some amazing experiences along the way.

I remember my first roundtable well. We were gathered together for the release of a film starring Pierce Brosnan. I had no idea what a roundtable was or what to do there. I asked the journalists present if we went around the table and each got to ask a question. That's how naive I was. I had been writing features and reviews and doing interviews for quite a while, but this was my first "roundtable." I learned rather quickly that it was a competitive game. If you wanted to ask a question, you had to jump in as soon as there was a pause in the conversation. If you didn't, someone else would. Later, when my colleagues and I were reminiscing about that day, one told me I looked like a deer in the headlights. But I learned quickly and was soon able to navigate this interview format with ease.

"Entertainment journalists can't survive without publicists, and publicists can't survive without them," said Jeff Hare, a publicist for DreamWorks (and formerly Warner Bros.) when we spoke in preparation for this book. While journalists and publicists can be rude to each other, thinking their time is more important than the time of others, they exist in a symbiotic relationship essential to the entertainment industry. Jeff, incidentally, is an outstanding publicist and the salt of the earth as a friend.

Publicists, while sometimes seen by journalists as the gatekeepers who prevent them from doing their jobs, are an essential part of the entire system and often go above and beyond the call of duty. Sometimes they'll partner with journalists and get great results. "I remember working with a journalist on a story with the bartending consultant of a film," Jeff said as he related a fun incident. "The interview was to be a bit of a pub crawl to get the real feel of what the consultant does for a living and subsequently for the film. By the end of the interview, the consultant, the journalist, and I were tanked. But the story came out great!"

While publicists can be friendly, they are gatekeepers of sorts, and an entertainment journalist would be wise to treat them well. I was curious to find out if celebs and filmmakers ever discuss entertainment journalists with the publicists, so I asked Jeff. "Of course," was his response. "All it takes is one negative experience with a journalist, and an actor or filmmaker will never forget him or her. There are those journalists that make people run and hide for fear of their poison pens. On the flip side, there are the journalists that are so talent-friendly that fingers get crossed that they'll be assigned to certain stories."

After you get the hang of working in an unfamiliar format and navigating the industry with publicists, the job of an entertainment journalist is definitely interesting and affords a lot of unique experiences. Imagine sitting across the aisle from Michael Eisner, then-CEO of The Walt Disney Company, at the first screening of the 2003 movie, *Pirates of the Caribbean,* and watching him make notes during the film. I have always wondered what he was writing.

And talking about unique experiences, two of the best happened to be at Disneyland. The first was the kickoff of the year leading to the 50th Anniversary of the park. Along with several dozen other journalists, I was allowed into the park before it even opened for the ceremony, which named Julie Andrews as the Honorary Ambassador for Disneyland's Golden Anniversary.

Then a year later, in 2005, I was once again given a special day at Disneyland on the anniversary. Besides a grand tour of the park—the insides and the outsides of the attractions—I saw Walt Disney's private apartment and never had to wait in line for an attraction. We went to the front of the line. And, hang onto your hats, I even had lunch with Michael Eisner, who was always one of the most gracious and endearing men whose company I have had the pleasure of. His enthusiasm for all things Disney is truly contagious. He is definitely someone I miss coming into contact with.

I have made many friends in this job, both publicists and journalists. I found over the years that some of the best parts of movie junkets are kibitzing with the other journalists. And many of the Television Critics Association Press Tours would have been totally boring had it not been for the company of my friends and colleagues. We have all shared some fun times and inside jokes.

There is one thing I might have done differently. I would have been more comfortable writing under a pseudonym; however, many outlets don't allow that and insist their writers use their real names. I'm not one of those people who needs to see their name in print. I do this job for the enjoyment—and, of course, the paycheck. But the work and final products are what drive me, not the fact that my name is on a byline.

While there are more than a few gray hairs that have sprouted on my head as a result of this job, there are even more good memories. The set visits, the one-on-ones, the junkets, the screenings, the phoners, the roundtables, the press conferences, and the friendships all add up to an interesting job that I have truly enjoyed. And, in a nutshell, that is what we all think! Here are some final thoughts from the contributors of this book:

George Pennacchio, KABC-TV

People often tell me how much they'd love to have my job—until they learn it's often filled with 10-plus hours plus regular work on the weekends seeing movies, interviewing the stars of those movies, covering awards shows, etc. It will never be a Monday through Friday, 9-to-5 job. It requires commitment, dedication, and a lot of hard work. You better love it. And I do.

Michael Lee, RadioFree.com

It may come with its own unique brand of poverty and stress that can only be appreciated by fellow reporters, but entertainment journalism has been, for me, a great experience to meet interesting and like-minded people. This job has exposed me to people from other cultures and their diverse perspectives, and I feel as though I have a better sense of the world community beyond the U.S. And in the final analysis, the pros overwhelm the cons: the freedom outweighs the deadlines, the creativity outweighs the long hours, and the friends outweigh the evil monkeys out to destroy you.

Fred Topel, Crave Online

I truly think this is the best job ever. I love movies and TV and being around them, so to be a part of the business in this capacity is fantastic. I have a role in every movie or TV show that comes out—a small role, a role towards the end when it's being released, but I'm involved.

Rick Bentley, *Fresno Bee*

There is no job in journalism that will touch as many people as writing about entertainment. It cuts across all demographics. And everyone always has an opinion they love to share.

Rob Owen, *Pittsburgh Post-Gazette*

The thing that I learned very quickly is that interviewing celebrities by and large is not that interesting. The people who I really enjoy interviewing are the people who create the shows and the people who run the shows. They are more honest. They are more forthcoming. A lot of time they have more thoughts in their head to express than the people that you see on-screen. Not always, but more often than not. I get better interviews with the people behind the scenes than I do with the stars. And I'm not sure that everyone appreciates that maybe it's not the star who's going to give you the best interview.

Howard Benjamin, Interview Factory Radio Networks

I had more fun at this than a human should be allowed, so if you need more stories, my memoirs are writing themselves every day. Just be patient—I'm not through, yet! I've made it clear to all the publicists that I've dealt with over the years that when I finally die, I expect them to chip in for my gravestone. On it, I want inscribed, "Can I have another five minutes?"

Donna Plesh, Thecolumnists.com

Well, I guess it would be a comment my college roomie made to me one day after I became a television writer. She remarked that one of our mutual friends "got paid to watch people knock small white balls into a hole" (he was a golf writer) and that I "got paid to watch television."

Scott Pierce, *Salt Lake Tribune*

I used to love it when Ted Turner came to the TCA Press Tour for interviews. It was a guaranteed column full of great stuff. He did, after all, once compare the plight of Turner Broadcasting to the Jews in Europe under Hitler and said he wished he owned nuclear weapons for use against Rupert Murdoch.

I was once invited to a Turner Classic Movies lunch and found myself seated next to Cheryl Crane, who is Lana Turner's daughter. We chatted amicably through the meal, and only slowly did I recall Crane's story. She stabbed her mother's gangster boyfriend, Johnny Stompanato, to death when she was only 14. (It was later ruled justifiable homicide.)

How cool is that?

Julio Martinez, *VIP Latino Magazine*, KPFK Radio

In 2000, as a theater critic for *Daily Variety*, I was assigned to review a one-person play called *My Big Fat Greek Wedding*, written and performed by unknown Nia Vardalos, performing at the 99-seat Globe Playhouse in West Hollywood. I loved the show, gave it a great review, and then invited Nia to be a guest on my radio show. Three years later, at a press conference announcing the hit film version of her show was being made into a CBS sitcom, Vardalos spotted me and pointed, "He's the guy. Julio was the first person in this town to notice me." That was nice.

Meg Mimura, *Lighthouse*

When I got into the Television Academy (ATAS), I bought a ticket to attend the Primetime Emmy Awards. Going to the Emmys had been my dream for a long time, but unfortunately the show was cancelled twice due to the aftermath of 9/11. I was very disappointed, but I guess it wasn't meant to be. Several years later, I was invited to the show by a Japanese publisher. I had to file my article in a few hours after the show. I rushed home and wrote an article from all the notes I jotted down during my attendance. I didn't have time to watch the DVR recording, but I believe it was the first posted comment about the Emmys in Japanese.

Since then, I've been attending the Emmys every year, thanks to a Japanese broadcaster, but I always come home disappointed. Who would have thought there is a much better way to approach the stars than going to the Emmys! The TCA press tours, international press junkets, studio tours, and electronic one-on-ones spoiled me to no end. Once you have easy access to practically anybody in the industry, going to an award show is nothing but frustration after frustration because the stars (so-to-speak) are heavily guarded.

My point is that you'll never know what tickles your fancy until you experience so many different aspects of this industry.

Margie Barron, *Production Update*

I want to add that I am horrified that "journalists" think they can ask the most personal questions—questions that they never, ever would ask their closest friends or relatives. I do not think it is okay to ask them to expose themselves. If the celebrity wants to talk about his or her personal life, fine, but the public does not have a right to know everything about a person.

When I interview young performers, I tell them up-front, if I ask a question and they don't want to answer, it's okay to say, "That's personal."

Brian Sebastian, Movie Reviews & More

In this business, "It's a marathon, not a sprint," and "There's no show without the business."

Stephen Whitty, *Star-Ledger*

At this point in my career, I'm lucky enough to be able to choose whom I want to interview, and as I'm generally writing long-ish Sunday stories, I get to concentrate on someone of interest to me.

You always have to serve the readers first, of course, and occasionally that means writing about currently popular stars who may not have a lot to say. But the best part of this job has been sitting down with people who have had long and varied careers—Pacino, Martin Scorsese, Kirk Douglas—and hearing how they do what they do so brilliantly.

Dave Walker, *New Orleans Times-Picayune*

It's just TV, but I'm pretty serious about what I do. I think navigation is an important role given the incredible amount of programming that's out there and the amount of time people spend in front of the tube. Steering a few readers to the stuff I think is worth their time is a good day's work. Covering the medium as a business—though more challenging than just passing judgment on show quality—is also an important part of the job. Accordingly, I wish I'd taken more business and math classes in college. And watched more TV.

Gerri Miller, Freelance

I wouldn't trade this job for anything!

Francine Brokaw

Well, you've almost come to the end of this book. So, what have you learned about being an entertainment journalist? Hopefully you now understand that it requires a lot of time and work and is a very competitive business. As Candace Havens stated, "There are few jobs and many entertainment journalists/critics." Don't forget the warning from Gerri Miller who said, "Only the strong survive." Mike Reynolds avowed that "this is a 24/7 profession." And "people have no idea how much time we invest in our craft," Brian Sebastian stated bluntly, which is a fact echoed throughout this book. So if you are not willing to put in the time, forget about it!

Also you should realize by now, if you didn't know this before, that celebrities are human beings with flaws just like the rest of us. Why people idolize them is beyond my comprehension. Some come into interviews looking like they just mowed the backyard. Some come in with alcohol on their breath or, worse yet, with a can of beer in their hand or glassy eyes and are unable to focus or make much sense. Others surprise us with how fun and friendly they are. The bottom line is: they are not their on-screen characters. They are regular human beings with good and bad aspects, just like you and me.

If you aspire to do this job, remember what you've read in this book. It is not all fun and games. "Entertainment takes over your world," Hanh Nguyen explained. "It's hard to turn it off." It requires a lot of discipline and patience. But—and this is a big "but"—it is also a lot of fun. And, as you've read, we have all experienced some pretty cool things in this job. However, that all comes *after* the hard work, long hours, and oftentimes a lot of stress.

Even though it is a competitive business, the fact that these journalists agreed to be interviewed for this book proves that we are a good bunch of people who were brought together because of our jobs and have ultimately become friends. If you think we should have our own reality series, you're right. We're just as entertaining, fun, and funny as the people in the hair and nail salon shows!

Now you know we don't spend our days lolling around with celebrities, and most of us are not on nightly national entertainment shows. We are hardworking journalists who just happen to be reporting on the entertainment business. We really like what we do. Yes, it is difficult at times, and yes, it is all-consuming, but it does have its moments. These moments are what keep us going, and going, and going.

Acknowledgments

I owe my sincere appreciation to all the journalists and publicists who took part in this project. While they are listed in this book with their current affiliation, many of them have been in this business long enough to have accrued a long list of credits. To include their resumes would not even do them justice. These hardworking and dedicated professionals whom I call my friends are truly a large part of the foundation on which the world of entertainment journalism stands today. Thank you all. (Aaron Barnhart, Margie Barron, Howard Benjamin, Rick Bentley, Winnie Bonelli, Jacqueline Cutler, Sean Daly, Todd Gilchrist, Jeff Hare, Candace Havens, Michael Lee, Julio Martinez, Valerie Milano, Gerri Miller, Meg Mimura, Hanh Nguyen, Rob Owen, George Pennacchio, Scott Pierce, Donna Plesh, Rob Salem, Mike Reynolds, Tim Riley, Brian Sebastian, David Sheehan, Bonnie Siegler, Alex Strachan, Fred Topel, Dave Walker, Stephen Whitty)

I also want to thank my editor, Amy Cook, who was supportive throughout this entire project and became a good friend.

This book is meant to entertain (a lot) as well as educate (a little) about what entertainment journalists do and what we have experienced. If you're looking for a great literary masterpiece, you'll have to wait for my next book!

And one final note: since people think we are friends with those we have interviewed—I'll be at your house for dinner a week from Thursday, George Clooney! And Portia and Ellen, pencil me in for Saturday. Sir Anthony Hopkins, how about Sunday brunch?

Index

Note: Because of the media's use of both first and last names for identification of celebrities and journalists, names are indexed by first name.